Laurence Jourdan

HOW TO CROCHET
CUTE ANIMALS

A Step-by-Step Guide with 15 Patterns

LOM
ART

INTRODUCTION

For longer than I'd care to recall, I really struggled with crochet. I simply couldn't find my way, and words like 'treble crochet' made me run a mile. But during lockdown something changed and my passion was born. I quickly created my pattern, a doll named Naelle. But it was Barney, my gentle bunny, who really made me delve deep into the world of crochet, notably thanks to his success with my social media community. I still can't quite believe it!

This book is a wonderful opportunity for me to share with you everything I've learned, all of my experiments and to try and make the jargon as easy to understand as possible. I will explain the basic techniques, and provide a few handy tips and tricks as well as some step-by-step patterns. If you are a beginner, be sure to watch online videos, as these are extremely helpful.

And for practice, I have created some simple and cute animals, a handful of tiny cuddly toys, neither too realistic nor too quirky. Every one of them holds a special place in my heart, whether from their initial design, as they were being created, or even when I was stitching in the final details on their faces. Each has its own character and story. Deep down in my heart, they are all alive! I wouldn't be surprised to see them get up and dance around.

Each of my designs can be created from head to toe and involve stitching very few seams. I prefer the technique of assembling each part using crochet alone. The animals are each categorized on the basis of their difficulty, from the simplest to the more difficult.

I sincerely hope you will find as much joy and satisfaction as I have in bringing life to the little animals you will find in this book, and nothing would make me happier than to see your final creations on social media. Simply post your pictures using the #lemondedesdoudousaucrochet hashtag so I can easily find and share them with everyone.

Happy crocheting, and more importantly, have fun!!
Laurence

Instagram: @arkidee.fr
www.arkidee.com

CONTENTS

WHAT YOU WILL NEED

GETTING STARTED

BASIC STITCHES

TECHNIQUES

Bonnie, Bella and Birdie,
the bunny sisters

62

Basil,
the bouncy bear

66

Hermione,
the wise lioness

70

Pinky,
the clever pig

74

Adrienne,
the musical elephant

78

Horace,
the hungry hippo

84

Millie and Tilly,
the shy tortoises

90

Baz and Gaz,
the chirpy birds

96

Freddie,
the funny fox

100

Snowflake, the skating
penguin

104

Oscar,
the busy beaver

110

Donnie,
the romantic donkey

116

Ricky, Nicky and Micky,
the naughty kittens

122

Zebby,
the pretty zebra

128

Hector,
the happy hound

134

« CROCHET CAN ALMOST BE SUMMED UP IN THREE EASY STEPS: FIRST YOU INSERT THE CROCHET HOOK, YARN OVER AND THEN PULL UP A LOOP. »

The
BASICS

YARN

Cotton, wool, alpaca wool, fancy yarn, fine, medium ... Where do you start?
In fact, it all depends on the desired effect and purpose.

Type of material

• **Cotton:** to make cuddly toys or *amigurumi* for babies, cotton is the ideal material. It does not lose fibres and is non-allergenic. In general, it is also much more rigid, which will stop it from looking worn out over time.

• **Other plant-based fibres:** linen and hemp are useful options, but not yet widely available. They are often blended with other fibres. Bamboo, which is very soft, has the disadvantage of lacking solidity.

• **Wool:** sheep's wool is soft, flexible and aerated, but can be a little coarse to the touch and some people do not like the feeling. Merino wool is very soft and does not cause any irritation.

• **Alpaca wool:** this is a very high-quality material. It is extremely soft, and non-allergenic, as it does not contain any lanolin. Its appearance gives off a very realistic furry texture, perfect for creating animals. Wool and alpaca wool need to be hand-washed. For babies, these materials should only be used for decorative bedroom items.

• **Fancy yarns and synthetic yarns:** these may be esthetically appealing (silk effect, soft, furry or bushy, etc.), but some can be quite difficult to use with crochet. I tend to avoid them.

DID YOU SAY 'AMIGURUMI'?

This is a portmanteau word taken from the Japanese word *ami* ('crocheted' or 'knitted') and *nuigurumi* ('cuddly toy'). An *amigurumi* can in fact be an animal, an object or a creature ... provided it is miniature. The cuteness of the final design is further emphasized with the addition of bodily features, such as facial details.

Weight of yarn

Just imagine yourself in a yarn shop! All of the balls of yarn in front of you are 50 g, but when you look a little more closely at the labels, the length (of the yarn) is not the same. Why? This is due to the weight of the yarn. The finer and lighter the yarn, the longer it will be. The ratio between weight/length of a yarn will determine its total weight.

The Craft Yarn Council (representing the primary yarn producers, accessories manufacturers, magazines, book publishers and consultants in the yarn industry) has drawn up an international classification for standard weights. As a result, on the vast majority – alas, not all – of yarn labels, you can easily see the category of the yarn. Those categories which are the most useful for us are the following:

Name	Category (US/UK – AU/NZ)		Length per 50 g	Needle size
Fine	Sport	5 Ply	150 to 200 m	3.25-3.75 mm (US D-F)
Light	DK Double Knit	8 Ply	100 to 150 m	3.75-4.5 mm (US F-7)
Medium	Worsted	10 Ply	60 to 100 m	4.5-5.5 mm (US 7-I/9)

WHAT IF THERE IS NO CATEGORY DISPLAYED?

If the category of yarn is not indicated on the label, the length and size of needles are given as a guide.

The weight of yarn to use will inevitably depend on the size of your creation. It is, therefore, important to make a clear distinction between the various weights available. **Fine** yarns are better suited to *amigurumi*, while **medium** yarns are more suitable for larger cuddly toys. For beginners, it is better to choose a lighter coloured, well-twisted yarn and **light** (Phildar Coton 3 is what I used when first starting out), or even medium (Phildar Coton 4). The yarn will not split and you will be able to clearly distinguish each stitch.

« To create my little animals, I primarily use extra soft **Krea Deluxe (fine) organic cotton**. I fully subscribe to their esthetic and ethical values (namely respect and consideration of the environment, people and animals). You can, of course, use any other yarns by using the colours of my creations as inspiration, or let your own creativity run free. Since these are only miniatures, you can create two to three animals with a single ball of yarn or even use any half-finished yarns.

« For all of the designs in this book, I have indicated the weight and length necessary. These indications correspond to the yarn and the crochet hook size used and my crochet method.

CROCHET HOOK

A crochet hook is made up of a hooked head and a shank with or without
a handle. This allows you to yarn over a stitch (or loop), hook the yarn
to pull it through the loop and then form another loop.

Crochet hooks come in a variety of **different materials** including metal and plastic (with or without an easy-grip handle), wood, bamboo etc. as well as **different sizes** (as a standard, hook sizes are given in metric units (for instance 2 mm etc) but in the US there may also be letter/numbers given instead).

There is nothing like a good tool, so be sure to choose one that suits you best! I recommend starting with a 3 mm hook and adjusting accordingly based on the guidance below.

❮❮ During my first attempts, I used a very fine crochet hook made from metal, similar to those which are often given away with crochet sets in stores. The tip was poorly made. I then bought a bamboo crochet hook, but the tip broke. I was then delighted to stumble across crochet hooks with easy-grip handles, much better suited to fit in the hand for ease of use. Some are even made from an opaque material which reduces reflection and is easier on the eyes.

For a single yarn, it is possible to use several different crochet hook sizes:

• A **finer crochet hook** will form much smaller and tighter stitches, and make the creation much more rigid (*amigurumi*).

• A **larger hook** will lead to larger and more flexible stitches, and the creation will be less rigid (clothing).

The size of the crochet hook can also be used to correct a crochet style. If you tend to produce stitches that are too tight, you could try a larger hook, and if your stitches are not tight enough, you could go for a finer hook.

WHAT'S THE BEST CROCHET HOOK SIZE FOR SOFT TOYS?

The hook size indicated on the soft toy label is given as a reference for crocheting clothing. However, to create your own *amigurumi*, you will need a smaller crochet hook than that, to avoid the stuffing from being visible or from coming out from between the stitches. For example, when it is recommended to use a 3 mm or 3.5 mm crochet hook, I tend to go for a 2.5 mm hook, or even a 2.25 mm when using cotton yarn. If you are working with wool, a 2.75 mm or 3 mm hook will allow you to retain a fuller finish.

OTHER TOOLS
AND A FEW USEFUL TIPS

• **A pair of scissors:** any that you already have or some very fine scissors, such as embroidery scissors, are ideal.

• **A yarn needle:** round-tipped, to easily pass through stitches without separating the loops (for instance, when fastening off the yarn).

• **An embroidery needle:** with a pointed tip and an eye wide enough to allow the yarn to pass through (to embroider eyes, nose or for other stitches such as the ears).

• **Large-headed sewing pins:** these will help you to avoid getting lost as you crochet (to mark points before embroidering or to keep items in the correct position before sewing).

• **Stitch markers:** these are sections of yarn in a different colour, a small safety pin or some form of marker. They should be placed at the start of each round.

• **A stuffing tool:** I use a wooden stick, but it is possible to use a pencil (the non-writing end). For very small creations, fine-tipped pliers could even be used.

• **Stuffing material:** polyester wadding in the form of cotton wool balls ideally. I tend to opt for Oeko-Tex material, which is guaranteed to be free of any toxins. It is useful to note that, typically, products labelled as 'anti-mite' and 'fire-resistant' have been made using a specific chemical. To limit the amount of filling and make my toys softer than those typically available, I only partially stuff them.

• **A notebook:** to note down all stages and stitches to be completed, and to tick them off as you go.

'SAFETY' EYES

These are plastic eyes with a toothed rod which can be inserted into your creation. A small disc then clips onto the end of the stick to hold the eye in place. Personally, I have chosen not to use these as I try to limit or avoid plastic altogether where possible. Also, if they are not properly inserted or break they can be dangerous, or pose a choking hazard. Do not use if the soft toy is to be used by a child under 3 years old.

TERMS AND
ABBREVIATIONS USED

Stitch: a completed combination of movements made by hooking loops through each other. Only finished once one loop remains on your hook.

Chain: refers to a single chain or collection of chain stitchs (See p. 30).

Loop: the yarn on your hook, section of yarn or section of a stitch (front loop, back loop).

Top of stitch: the upper section of a stitch formed of two horizontal loops (front loop and back loop) that looks like a V shape.

Row: a line formed by stitches.

Round: a collection of crochet stitches in a round or spiral formation.

Crochet in rows: the 1st row is crocheted on the base of a chain. At the end of each row, you insert the hook and turn the creation around to begin crocheting directly above the previous row (See p. 18).

Crochet in a round: working around a magic ring, stitch or chain. All rounds are closed by a slip stitch.

Crochet in a spiral: working around a magic ring, stitch or chain, but the rounds are not closed off. The creation resembles a perfect spiral.

Insert the hook: inserting the point of the hook (See p. 22).

Yarn over: rolling the yarn around the shank of the crochet hook from the back, over the top to the front.

Yarn under: rolling the yarn around the shank of the crochet hook from the front, underneath to the back.

Pull up a loop: with the hooked end of the crochet hook, draw the yarn through a stitch.

Front, back: the front (or outside of the creation) is the visible side, the most attractive to look at. The back is the hidden side, the inside.

V-stitch or X-stitch: on the front of the creation, single crochet stitches look like the letter V or the letter X (See p. 32).

Fastening off: making a knot and/or weaving in your ends (See p. 52).

Weaving in ends: hiding the yarn.

sc: single crochet (UK double crochet, dc)

hdc: half-double crochet (UK half-treble crochet, htr)

dc: double crochet (UK treble crochet, tr)

sl st: slip stitch

ch: chain stitch

dec: decrease

inc: increase

BLO: back loop only

FLO: front loop only

st: stitch

Rnd: round

... x ...: repeat the pattern as many times as indicated. For example: *1 sc, 1 inc* x 2. You will crochet 1 sc, 1 inc, 1 sc, 1 inc.

= ... st(s): total number of stitches.

 : difficulty level.

HOW TO HOLD
THE HOOK AND YARN

Right-handed people will hold the hook with the right hand, and the yarn with the left. Left-handed people will work in the other direction.

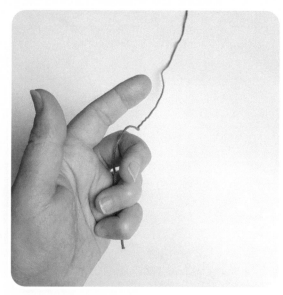

There is no right way to hold your hook and yarn. Some people (myself included) hold it using the pencil grip, between the thumb and index finger, with the handle pointed upwards. Others hold it using the knife grip, with the handle in their hand.

To hold the yarn, the most important thing to remember is to feel comfortable and keep the tension. Some people prefer to wrap it around several fingers or just one finger, others prefer to keep their index finger pointed outwards.

I tend to work as you can see in the picture. I hold the yarn using my ring finger and little finger pressed into my palm and use the middle finger of my left hand to adjust the tension. This allows me to hold my creation between my left thumb and index fingers.

WHAT IS THE PURPOSE OF KEEPING THE RIGHT TENSION?

The yarn tension plays a very important role. It determines your crochet style and has a direct impact on the overall result of your work. When you are first starting out, you will either pull too tight, or not tight enough, and the crochet stitches will not be the same throughout.

Be sure to practice and do some test runs. You will find the crochet style which suits you best and learn to adjust any problems.

⫷ A note for left-handed people

If you are a left-handed person and just starting out, you may have some difficulty initially in understanding the basic photos and crochet techniques since they show someone using their right hand.

Here are a couple of tips to help you along:

• Place the book in front of a mirror to look at the photos

• Take a photo of the images and flip them horizontally to mirror the images.

STARTING
TO CROCHET

The slip knot

The most basic crochet technique is the chain. Whether crocheting in rows or in the round,
your piece may start with a chain. They are also used throughout pieces to help create shapes.
Your first loop is made using a slip knot.

There are several methods to creating a slip knot. This is how I do it:

1. Make a loop by placing the piece of yarn leading to the ball on top of the end of the piece of yarn. Leave yourself a long tail end to make sure nothing comes undone.

2. Insert the hook through the loop.

3. Take the piece of yarn closest to the ball and pull it through the loop, making sure not to pull through the yarn tail through the loop. You will then have a loop around the hook with a knot beneath it.

4. Tighten the knot by pulling on the yarn tail. Now you are ready to begin your chain.

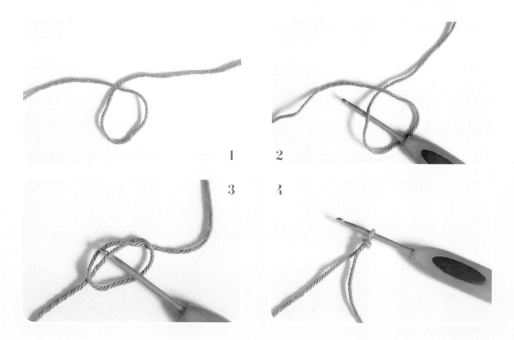

The magic ring

The magic ring is ideal for a piece of crochet where the centre point
needs to be completely closed off. This is the starting point for working
as a round (with closed edges) or as a spiral (with open edges).

A magic ring (otherwise known as a magic circle or loop) allows you to both create the first loop on your hook and crochet the stitches for your first round. The fact that it is adjustable means you can tighten it as you go by pulling on the end of the yarn, to avoid leaving a hole in the centre (this is important if you are going to stuff your final creation).

It may be standard (1 loop around your finger) or double (2 loops around your finger). Let me share my easy-to-follow method:

1. Take the end of the yarn in your hand and wrap the yarn around your index finger (over and under, and then over again), making sure the piece of yarn closest to the ball is on top.

2. Slide the crochet hook beneath the first loop (closest to the end of the yarn), and then take the yarn closest to the ball and draw it beneath the loop. You will then have a loop on the crochet hook. You can now remove your finger from the ring, as I have done here, and hold it between your thumb and index finger.

3. Yarn over. Then draw the yarn through the loop on the hook.

4. You will then have a loop which will allow the magic ring to be used for the first single crochet stitches of the round. Do not count this as a stitch.

1

2

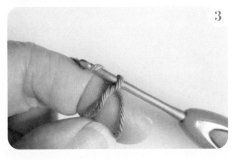
3

4

1ˢᵀ ROUND IN THE MAGIC RING USING SINGLE CROCHET STITCHES:

1. Insert the crochet hook through the ring, and yarn over.

2. Draw the yarn through the ring. You will then have 2 loops on your crochet hook.

3. Yarn over and draw the yarn through the 2 loops on your crochet hook.

4. Your first double crochet stitch is now complete.

5. Crochet as many stitches as indicted in the pattern. To finish, pull the end of the yarn to tighten the ring.

6. You can now start the 2ⁿᵈ round.

If your pattern calls for joined rounds, you will close the round off with a slip stitch into the top of the first st (not the chain). If you are working in continuous spirals, you will not.

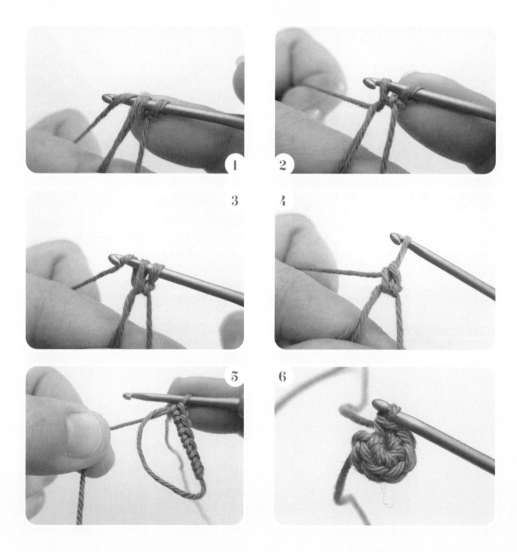

A HANDY TIP TO TIGHTEN THE MAGIC RING AND COMPLETELY CLOSE THE HOLE:

If you have used a single loop for your magic ring, as opposed to a double loop, to secure your yarn tail and stop it from coming undone, follow these steps on your second round:

1. Before trimming your yarn tail, hold it along the top-back of your stitches so as you insert your hook in the top of the stitches your hook is also beneath the yarn tail.

2. Then, crochet this along with the first 4 single crochet stitches on the 2nd round (See p. 32).

3. Tighten this once more by pulling on the end of the yarn.

4. Go all the way around with the end of the yarn, which will then be completely trapped by the stitches on the 2nd round. Cut off any excess. The hole will then be fully closed.

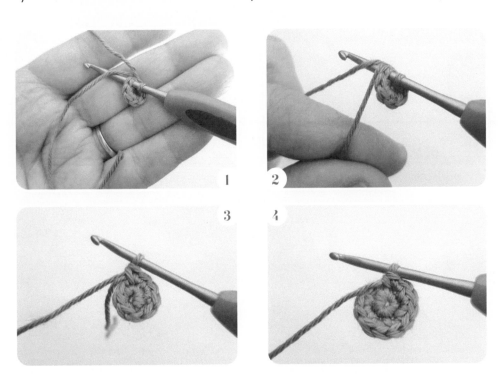

INSERTING
THE CROCHET HOOK

For beginners, this is not always easy to grasp, especially since it is possible to insert the crochet hook in different sections of your creation - for instance, beneath the 2 loops at the top of the stitch, beneath 1 loop only, in a previous row, etc.

Beneath both loops

Unless otherwise indicated in the patterns, you should insert the crochet hook beneath both loops at the top of the next stitch. Here are two examples.

WORKING IN THE ROUND:

WORKING IN ROWS:

Beneath the front loop

This technique is useful when creating an invisible decrease (see p. 37). It also allows an angle to be created on your creation to face forward. If indicated in the pattern, you should insert the crochet hook beneath the loop in front of the top of the next stitch.

‹‹ We use this method to create the fold between the torso and legs on the bunnies Bonnie, Bella and Birdie on p. 62 as well as the snout on Pinky the pig on p. 74.

Beneath the back loop

This technique creates a particular visual effect (a row of front loops) or a right angle for the crochet to bend backwards. You should insert the crochet hook beneath the back loop at the top of the next stitch down the middle of the stitch – this technique will be indicated in the pattern.

‹‹ We use this method for the legs and nose on Basil the bouncy bear on p. 66.

Around a chain

(See p. 30)

This technique allows you to create an oblong or long shape. On the 1ˢᵗ round, you need to insert the crochet hook into a single loop on both sides of the chain.

<<< We use this method for the nose on Horace the Hippo on p. 84 and the tails on Baz and Gaz the chirpy birds on p. 96.

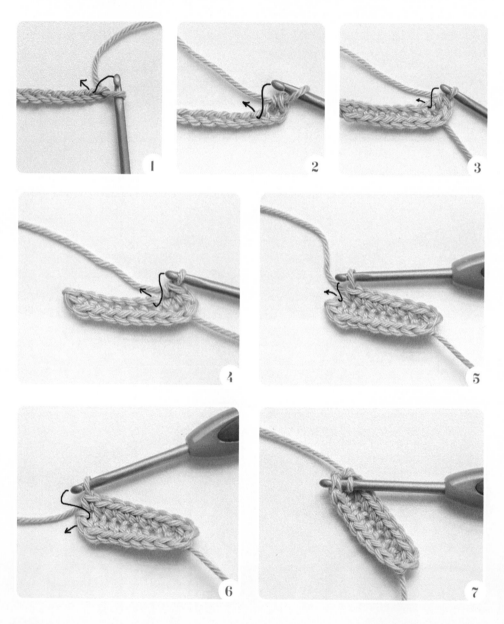

In a single loop on the chain

We use this method at the start of a crochet in rows, to create a string, for the animal's crotch, etc.

Working under the back bump

This technique gives you a much neater edging and is much prettier when starting your pattern.

1. On the front side of the chain, you can see a row of V-stitches formed by 2 loops.

2. When you turn the chain over, you will see the 3rd loop.

3. Do not over-tighten the chain so you can insert the crochet beneath this 3rd loop.

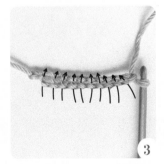

COUNTING STITCHES
AND ROWS

Crochet in a spiral, V-stitches

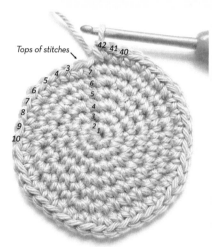

Tops of stitches

(See Basics, p. 32).

This circle is crocheted using V-stitches. It has 7 rounds.

The first stitches on each round, which are colour-coded and numbered, allow you to count the number of rounds from the centre of the circle.

To count the number of stitches from the last round, working around the edge of the circle, you should count the tops of the stitches (at the upper edge of the stitch), here is a total of 42 stitches

Crochet in a spiral, X-stitches

Tops of stitches

This circle is crocheted using X-stitches. It also has 7 rounds.

The first stitches on each round are colour-coded and numbered.

If you count the tops of stitches from the last round, there are also a total of 42 stitches.

Chain

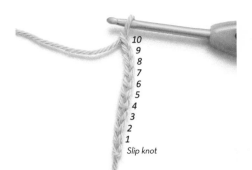

(See p. 30).

This chain has 10 chain stitches.

Do not count the slip knot, or the loop on your hook as a stitch.

Crochet in a row

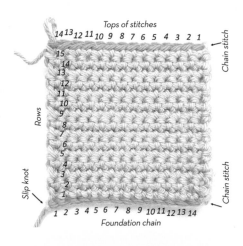

This piece is made using single crochet stitches, working in rows across 15 rows in total, from a chain with 14 chain stitches (+1 for your turning chain).

To know how many stitches are in each row, you need to count the tops of stitches (at the upper edge of the stitch).

In this example, there are 14 (the same number as chain stitches on the foundation chain).

There is no difference between front and back.

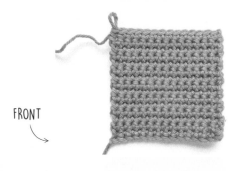

FRONT

BACK

The difference between the front and back

For a piece made in the round, the right side (the front of the piece/the visible side) and the wrong (or the inside) are always different.

Both of these circles are shown from the front. The design of the V-stitches (on the left) and X-stitches (on the right) is visible. This side of the design is much more attractive.

The back of both of these circles is clearly different from the front, with the appearance of horizontal lines at the tops of the stitches, making it appear more cluttered. It is possible to use this side on the outside, for a textured effect, but I don't recommend doing so with my patterns.

→» A USEFUL TIP «←

When you are crocheting a small, narrow piece in a spiral, such as an arm, ear or leg, the creation tends to curl in, meaning the front turns on the inside.

For your first few rounds, you must turn the creation the right way to avoid crocheting on the wrong side. If you don't do this, you will struggle to turn it right side out later on when crocheting my designs.

CROCHETING A
CHAIN (CH)

Yarn over and pull up a loop to form a chain

1. Yarn over (wrap the yarn over the crochet hook, from back to front).
2. Pull the yarn through the loop on the crochet hook.
3. This then creates a chain stitch.
4. Repeat as many times as indicated in the pattern to form a chain.

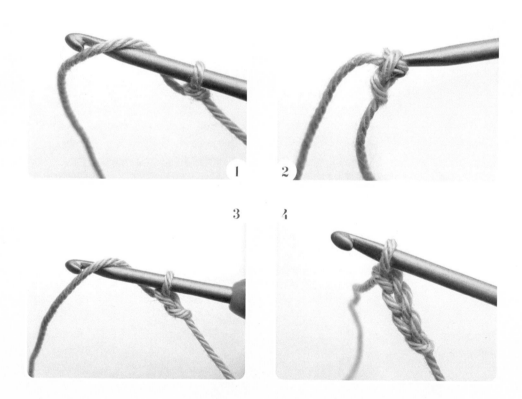

Chain stitch above a single crochet stitch

This process is used to create the animal's crotch for example.

1. Yarn over.

2. Draw the yarn through the loop on the crochet hook.

3. This then creates a chain stitch. Repeat as many times as indicated in the pattern.

3

SINGLE CROCHET STITCH (SC)

V-Stitch

1. Insert the hook into the next stitch, under both loops unless otherwise specified.
2. Yarn over.
3. Pull up a loop through the top of the stitch, you will have 2 loops left on your hook.
4. Yarn over.
5. Pull the yarn through the 2 remaining loops.
6. This then forms a single crochet V-stitch.

⇢ USEFUL INFO ⇠

My animals have all been made using V-stiches.

X-Stitch

1. Insert the hook into the next stitch, under both loops unless otherwise specified.
2. Yarn under (wrap the yarn under the crochet hook, from back to front).
3. Pull up a loop through the top of the stitch, you will have 2 loops left on your hook.
4. Yarn over (over the top of the crochet hook).
5. Pull the yarn through the 2 remaining loops.
6. This then forms a single crochet X-stitch.

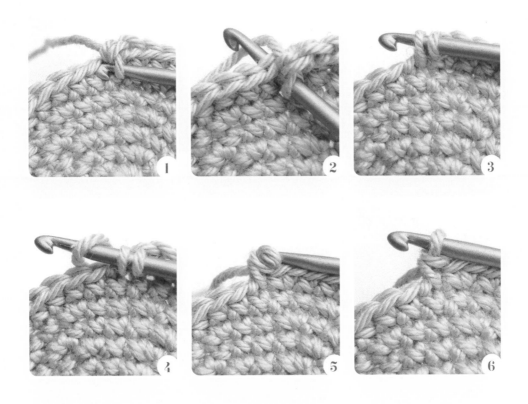

⇢⇢ USEFUL INFO ⇇⇇

X-stitches are tighter than V-stitches,
creating a smaller and more rigid design.

SLIP STITCH (SL ST)

This stitch is multifunctional and can be used to fasten off a stitch or project, create a neat edge, create a cord, or create an invisible seam.

1. Insert the hook in the next stitch.
2. Yarn over.
3. Pull the yarn over through all the loops on your hook.
4. This then forms a slip stitch.

INCREASING
(INC)

An increase stitch means 2 crochet stitches in the same hole.

1. Insert the hook into the same stitch you just worked.

2. Yarn over and pull through.

3. Yarn over and pull the yarn through the 2 loops. You will then have 2 stitches in the same hole.

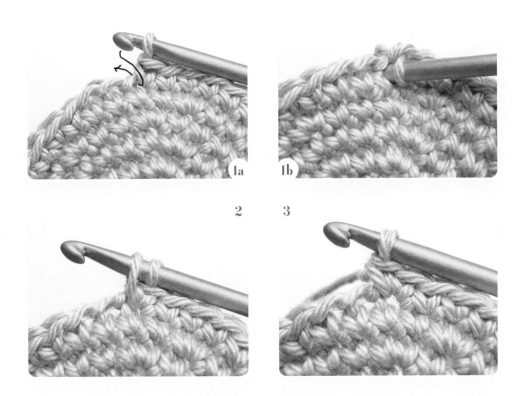

⇢ USEFUL INFO ⇠

Sometimes you will need a 3-stitch increase (in this instance you will need to crochet 3 stitches in the same hole). Half-double crochet or double crochet increases follow the same process with 2 or 3 stitches being crocheted into the same hole.

DECREASING (DEC)

A decrease stitch means reducing 2 stitches to one.

Decrease stitch

This technique consists of starting a single crochet before you combine it with the next stitch. Also referred to as a single crochet 2 together (sc2tog)

1. Insert the hook in the next stitch, yarn over and pulling up a loop. You will have 2 loops left on your hook.

2. Insert the hook in the next stitch, yarn over and draw the yarn through. You will have 3 loops left on your hook.

3. Yarn over.

4. Draw the yarn through all 3 remaining loops.

5. 2 stitchs from the previous row will now be joined into 1.

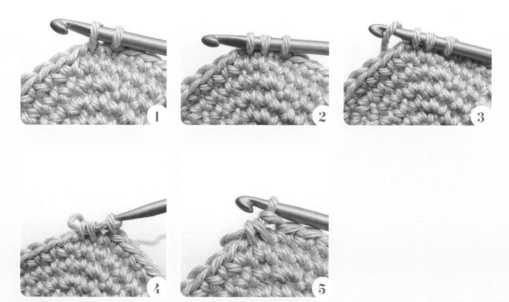

Invisible decrease

This technique consists of inserting the crochet hook only beneath the front loop of 2 stitches to combine them together, creating a seemingly invisible decrease.

1. Insert the hook beneath the front loop of the next stitch.
2. Then insert the hook beneath the front loop of the next stitch as well.
3. You will then have 3 loops on the hook. Yarn over.
4. Pull the yarn through the first 2 loops (the 2 front loops).
5. Yarn over.
6. Pull the yarn through the 2 loops. 2 stitchs from the previous row will now be joined into 1.

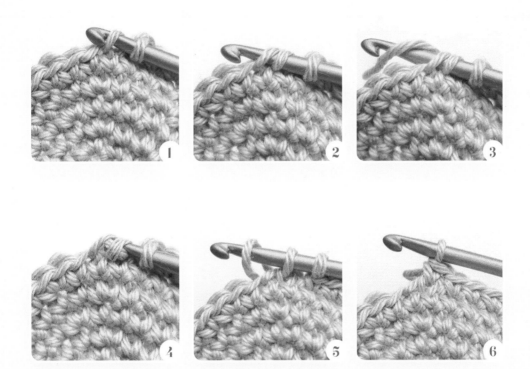

HALF-DOUBLE
CROCHET (HDC)

The half-double crochet (UK half-treble crochet) is slightly taller than the single crochet stitch.

1. Yarn over before you insert your hook.
2. Insert the hook in the next stitch.

3. Yarn over.

4. Pull the yarn through the top of the stitch. 3 loops will then be on the hook.

5. Yarn over.

6. Draw the yarn through the 3 loops.

7. A half-double crochet is then formed. Notice the difference in height compared to the double crochet to the right.

DOUBLE CROCHET
(DC)

The double crochet (UK treble crochet (tr)) is twice the height of a single crochet.

1. Yarn over before you insert your hook.
2. Insert the crochet hook in the next stitch.
3. Yarn over.
4. Pull the yarn through the top of the stitch. You will have 3 loops left on your hook.
5. Yarn over.
6. Draw the yarn through the first 2 loops.
7. 2 loops remain on the hook.

8. Yarn over.

9. Draw the yarn through the 2 loops.

10. A double crochet is then formed. To its right there is a half-double crochet and further right a single crochet. Notice the height difference between the 3 stitches.

CROCHETING A
PIECE CLOSED

When you have finished crocheting a piece, such as an arm, tail or ear,
you sometimes need to close the opening. This can be done by stitching or crocheting
the single crochet stitches. I prefer the latter, making it easier to attach
the piece to the body or head (See p. 46).

Using the loop on the crochet hook, pinch together the top of the piece to flatten it and align the stitches of each side.

1. Insert the hook into the stitch at the front of the piece (beneath the two loops) and in the rear stitch opposite (beneath the two loops): you should now have 5 loops on the hook. Yarn over (wrap the yarn over the crochet, from back to front).

2. Pull the yarn through the first 4 loops.

3. Yarn over again.

4. Draw the yarn through the remaining 2 loops.

5. Repeat for the other stitches.

6. The piece is now closed off.

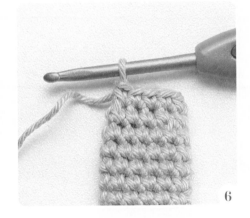

JOINING
THE LEGS

Assembling the legs using a chain fulfils 3 purposes: assembling,
creating a join between the legs, and beginning the body. Depending on the
number of chain stitches, the legs will be closer together or further apart.

Starting point: the 1st leg should be crocheted and then fastened off and left to one side.
The 2nd leg should be crocheted, but do not fasten off.

1. Start of the body on the 2nd leg: work single crochet stitches around the front of the
leg (total stitches are indicated on each pattern). Remember to put a stitch marker
into the first stitch. This means that the start of the rounds is on the outside of the leg.

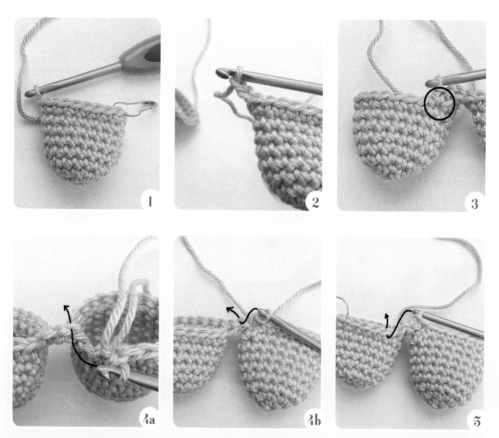

2. **From the 2nd leg,** crochet as many chain stitches as indicated in the pattern to form the crotch.

3. **Join to the 1st leg:** insert the 1st stitch into the stitch where the slip stitch was crocheted (at the end of the 1st leg). Crochet all stitches on the 1st leg.

4. **Crotch:** in this section, you need to insert the hook into a single loop on the chain stitches (arrow stitches) to separate the piece (create the back).

5. **Rear side of the 2nd leg:** from the arrow stitch, crochet stitches as far as the stitch marker.

6. **The first round of the body** is now complete.

7. **2nd round of the body:** crochet the front of the 2nd leg as far as the crotch. Crotch: crochet single crochet stitches in the other loop of the chain stitches (creation of the stomach).

8. **1st leg:** crochet single crochet stitches on the 1st leg, from the arrow stitch.

9. **Crotch and the rear side of the 2nd leg:** complete the second round as far as the marker.

10. **Finishing:** using the yarn left to one side at the end of the 1st leg, hide any holes in the crotch.

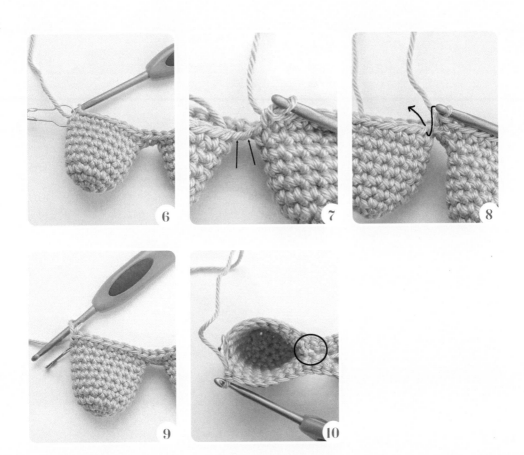

CROCHETING TWO
PIECES TOGETHER

This technique can be used to join together **arms**, **wings** and the **tail** to the body, and **ears** to the head. If you prefer to sew pieces on then you may do so.

Starting point: the arms (or wings, tail, ears) have been crocheted and placed to one side. You now need to join them to the body (or head).

1. Place the piece to be joined (shown in yellow on photo 1) in front of the body (or head) by aligning the stitches opposite each other. Make sure the pieces are the right way around on the animal, whether they need to be on the front or back (for example wings on a bird).

2. Insert the hook in the stitch on the piece to be joined under both loops and in the stitch on the body (or head). You now have 4 loops + 1 already on the crochet hook, meaning there are 5 loops overall.

3. Yarn over.

4. Pull the yarn through the first 4 loops.

5. Yarn over again.

6. Then draw the yarn through the 2 remaining loops.

7. Crochet the other stitches using the same technique. The 2 pieces will now be joined.

INVISIBLE FINISH

Finish your crocheted pieces neatly by using an invisible finish stitch, creating a fake top of stitch to hide the end of your round.

Stop the round

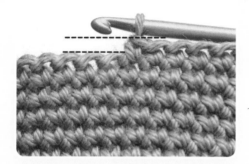

Where a piece crocheted in a spiral is finished, the end of the round is higher than the start of the round. It doesn't look very attractive.

1. To resolve this, crochet a slip stitch, cut the yarn and then draw it through the loop.

2. Then you can imitate a top of stitch as follows. Thread the yarn onto a yarn needle. Insert the needle beneath the 2 loops of the next stitch, from front to back (as if you were crocheting the stitch).

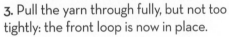

3. Pull the yarn through fully, but not too tightly: the front loop is now in place.

4. Insert the needle only beneath the rear loop of the slip stitch, with your needle point out the back.

5. Draw the yarn through fully: the rear loop is now in place.

6. Place the yarn through several rear stitches and secure it in place (See p. 52).

7. The end of the round is now invisible.

Close off a round

Starting point: on the penultimate round of the head, you have undertaken the last few decreases. There are now only 6 stitches left and an opening. To completely close off the piece, we will use a yarn needle to insert the yarn through each stitch. This technique will imitate a crocheted round, which counts as the last round.

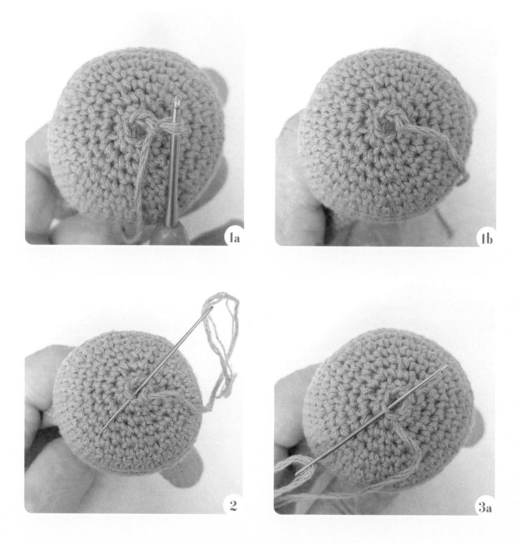

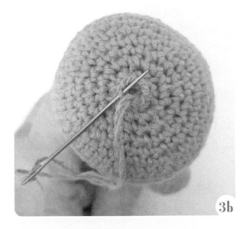

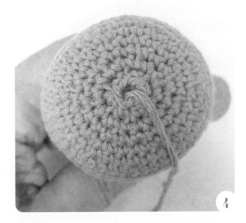

1. Fasten off leaving a 20 cm tail for weaving in.

2. Thread the yarn through the needle and insert the needle beneath the 2 loops of the next stitch, from the inside towards the outside.

3. Insert the needle beneath each loop in front of the next 5 stitches, from the outside towards the inside.

4. When you have completed the round, pull the end of the yarn to completely close the opening.

5. Weave in your end (See p. 52).

FINISHING OFF
AND WEAVING IN ENDS

At the end of a creation, embroidery or stitching, you need to secure both ends of the yarn and weave them in using a yarn needle.

End of a piece

1

Insert the needle through the stitches and make sure that you cannot see the yarn. Then weave the yarn through another row.

2

Insert the needle inside the piece, and bring it out at a different place.

3

Cut the yarn and weave the remaining end through so that it is no longer visible.

End of a creation

1. Insert the needle into the centre of the creation and pull it out at another place, in the middle of a stitch.

2. Insert the needle once more into the same place and pull it through elsewhere. Gently pull on the yarn so you can no longer see the loop. Repeat 2 to 3 times.

3. Cut the yarn and weave the remaining end through so that it is no longer visible.

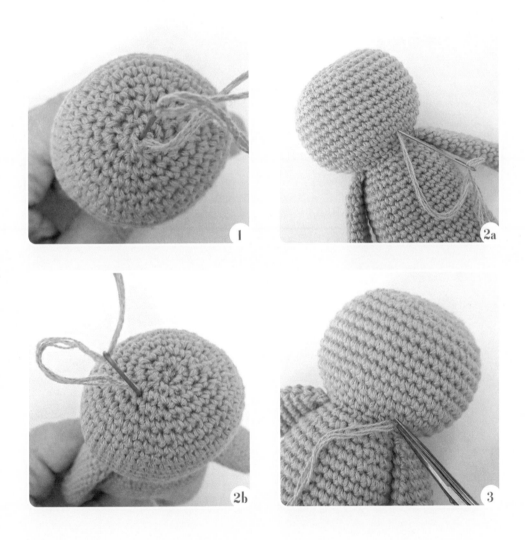

Fastening off embroidery

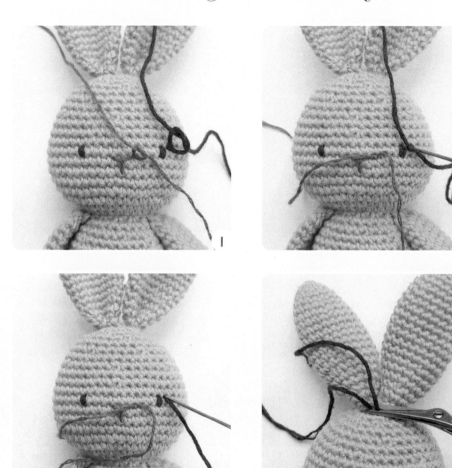

After stitching details on the surface of your project, both ends of the yarn will be visible on the right side of your work.

1. Tie a double knot with these two ends.

2. Insert the yarn at the same place as the knot.

3. Draw the yarn out elsewhere by pulling hard enough to hide the knot on the inside and cut off any excess.

After sewing on a piece

After sewing a piece such as a snout or muzzle, for example, you will only have one piece of yarn to fasten off. Make sure the knot is not visible, for instance by pulling through a stitch.

MAKE AN INVISIBLE KNOT

To tie a knot, insert the needle into the creation, form a loop, insert the needle through the loop and draw through. You can then hide the yarn inside the creation.

After sewing together two pieces

After having sewn on the ears for instance, you will then have two ends of yarn to fasten off. The principle is the same as after embroidery (see opposite).

Draw them through at the same place, in the middle of a stitch, and tie a double knot.

You can then hide the yarn inside the creation by weaving the ends in.

CHANGING YARN
AND/OR COLOUR

Whether you are at the end of a ball of yarn or you need to change the colour,
the method is identical. If you come to the end of a ball of yarn, you just
need to be sure to keep enough length for the change.

Making stripes

End of row in colour A:

1. Start the last single crochet. To do this, yarn over and pull through. Two loops in colour
A will then be on the hook.

Changing colour:

2. Using the yarn in colour B, draw over for the last time through the stitch and draw through the 2 loops on the hook.

3. Result: the last stitch on the row is now complete, in colour A, and the new yarn is on the hook.

4. Crochet the stitches on the row in colour B until the penultimate stitch on the row.

New colour change:

5 to 8. On the final stitch of the row, yarn over the first time in colour B and the last time in colour A.

◄◄ Both ends of the yarn will then be secured at the back.

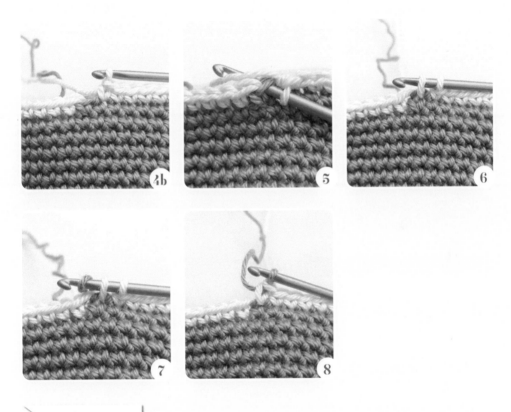

SPECIAL CASE

For more complex colour changes (circles or ovals), you sometimes need to plan the colour change 2 stitches in advance. This is notably the case for Hector the Happy Hound (p. 134), where detailed explanations are provided in the pattern.

STITCHING
SEAMS

Stitching an ear

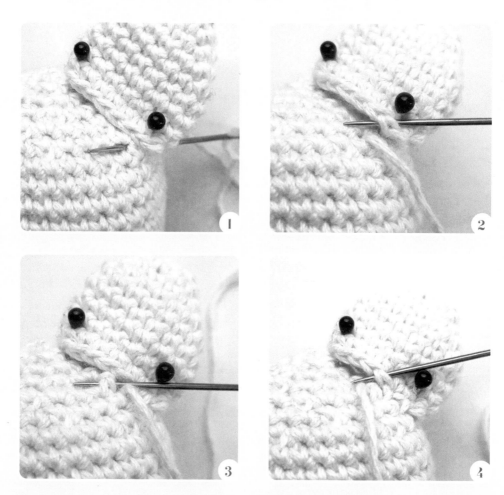

Place the ear in the correct position and fasten it in place using pins.

The ear should be sewn in place using the visible loop stitch and a yarn needle. To do this, insert the needle beneath a top stitch (photo 1), then beneath 2 loops (=top stitch on the ear) sideways on (photo 2). Repeat these stitches all the way around the ear (photos 3 and 4), as indicated in the patterns.

Sewing a flat ear and fastening off

Place the flat ear in position and fix using pins.

Follow the steps indicated above (using the **visible loop**), but insert the needle into the two thickest parts of the ear and fasten off. Do not go all the way around the ear so it stays flat.

Sewing a snout or muzzle

Also use an **visible loop** to sew on the snout or muzzle.

« TO CREATE A CROCHET CUDDLY TOY YOU
WILL NEED YOUR INNER CHILD, A LITTLE PATIENCE
AND A WHOLE LOT OF LOVE. SO, SNUGGLE UP IN YOUR
FAVOURITE COMFY CHAIR AND HAVE FUN! »

Crochet Animal
PATTERNS

THE BUNNY SISTERS ARE AROUND 19 CM TALL

BONNIE, BELLA AND BIRDIE
THE BUNNY SISTERS

Bonnie is the quiet one, Bella is the negotiator and Birdie
is the most outgoing. Their little fights never last long and are
quickly forgotten with endless laughs!

YOU WILL NEED:

1 x 2.25 mm crochet hook – Polyester wadding for stuffing
Krea Deluxe organic cotton yarn: 40 cm in Black 28 (eyes)
Bonnie: • 22 g or 73 m of Natural 01 (body),
40 cm of Earth Brown 29 (nose)
Bella: • 22 g of 73 m de Croissant 53 (body),
40 cm Earth Brown 29 (nose)
Birdie: • 22 g or 73 g of Cognac 52 (body),
40 cm of Croissant 53 (nose)

METHOD

→→ All of the pieces are crocheted in a spiral from a
magic ring.
→→ You should start by crocheting the arms and the
first leg to then be able to join to the body when
necessary. The second leg, body and head are then
crocheted without fastening off.
→→ The ears are the final piece to be crocheted.

BELLA

BIRDIE

BONNIE

⇒» 1. THE ARMS «⇐

You should begin by crocheting the arms without stuffing. Make 2.

Rnd 1: 6 sc into a magic ring. Pull ring closed.

Rnd 2: inc x 6 = 12 sts.

Rnd 3: 12 sc (11 rnds).

Rnd 14: *1 dec, 4 sc* x 2 = 10 sts.

Rnd 15: close the opening of the arm using 4 sc

Fasten off, leaving a 15 cm tail, weave in ends. Leave the arms to one side.

⇒» 2. THE LEGS «⇐

1ST LEG:

Rnd 1: 5 sc into a magic ring. Pull ring closed.

Rnd 2: inc x 5 = 10 sts.

Rnd 3: *1 sc, 1 inc* x 5 = 15 sts.

Rnd 4: *4 sc, 1 inc* x 3 = 18 sts.

Rnd 5 to 7: 18 sc (3 rnds).

Rnd 8: *4 sc, 1 dec* x 3 = 15 sts.

Finish with one sl st. Fasten off, leaving a 20 cm tail and put to one side.

2ND LEG:

Repeat as the 1st leg, but stop after round 8: do not crochet the slip stitch, do not fasten off.

⇒» 3. THE BODY «⇐

You can now begin the body by joining the legs. Place a stitch marker in the 1st stitch.

Rnd 9: 8 sc (front of the 2nd leg), 2 ch without tightening (=crotch), 15 sc (in the first leg), 23 sc (in only 1 loop of the 2 ch), 7 dc (back of the 2nd leg) = 34 sts.

Rnd 10: 8 sc, 2 sc (in the other loop of the 2 ch), 24 sc = 34 sts.

The stitch marker is on the side of the body.

On the next round, do not tighten the slip stitches.

Rnd 11: 2 sc, 5 sl st, 5 sc, 5 sl st, 17 sc = 34 sts.

Rnd 12: 2 sc, 5 sc in the front loops of the sl st, 5 sc, 5 sc in the front loops of the sl st, 17 sc. = 34 sts.

Rnd 13: 34 sc.

Rnd 14: 7 sc 1 inc 4 sc 1 inc 21 sc = 36 sts.

After the next row, use the yarn tail left from the 1st leg to hide any holes in the crotch. You can then stuff the legs. The body and head can be stuffed as you work or at the end, as you prefer.

Rnd 15 to 18: 36 sc (4 rnds).

Rnd 19: 4 sc, 1 dec, 11 sc, 1 dec, 17 sc = 34 sts.

Rnd 20 to 25: 34 sc (6 rnds).

Rnd 26: [*7 sc, 1 dec * x 3], 5 sc, 1 dec = 30 sts.

Rnd 27: 2 sc, 1 dec, [*6 sc, 1 dec * x 3], 2 sc = 26 sts.

Rnd 28: 2 sc, 1 dec, 12 sc, 1 dec, 8 sc = 24 sts.

You are now on the bunny's back. On the next round, you will crochet the arms to the body.

Rnd 29: 1 sc, 4 sts with first arm (for each sc, insert the hook in 1 st on the arm and 1 st on the body = 4 loops), 4 dec, 4 sc with the second arm (worked same as first arm), 3 dec. There will be 1 st left on the round = 17 sts.

Move the stitch marker to last stitch completed (= new starting point of the rounds), now crochet a 4th dec = 16 sts.

«⇐ Depending on how you crochet, the arms may appear a little off-centre. If so, you need to change their position, while keeping an identical number of stitches.

Rnd 30: 13 inc, 2 sc, 1 inc = 30 sts.

Finish stuffing the body. Do not fasten off.

⇢⇢ 4. THE HEAD ⇠⇠

Rnd 31: 2 sc, 1 inc, [*4 sc, 1 inc* x 5], 2 sc = 36 sts.

Rnd 32: *5 sc, 1 inc* x 6 = 42 sts.

Rnd 33: 7 sc, 1 inc, 10 sc, 1 inc, 10 sc, 1 inc, 12 sc = 45 sts.

Rnd 34 to 38: 45 sc (5 rnds).

Rnd 39: 8 sc, 1 dec, 10 sc, 1 dec, 10 sc, 1 dec, 11 sc = 42 sts.

Rnd 40: 42 sc.

Rnd 41: *5 sc, 1 dec* x 6 = 36 sts.

Rnd 42: 36 sc.

Rnd 43: 2 sc, 1 dec, [*4 sc, 1 dec* x 5] 2 sc = 30 sts.

Rnd 44: 30 sc.

Rnd 45: *3 sc, 1 dec* x 6 = 24 sts.

Rnd 46: 1 sc ,1 dec, [*2 sc, 1 dec* x 5], 1 sc = 18 sts.

Rnd 47: *1 sc, 1 dec* x 6 = 12 sts.

Finish stuffing the head.

Rnd 48: 6 dec = 6 sts.

Fasten off, leaving a 20 cm tail. Finish with an invisible finish and weave in ends.

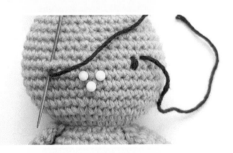

⇢⇢ 5. EYES AND NOSE ⇠⇠

The eyes are placed on a stitch on round 37 and have 8 stitches between them. Embroider 2 vertical points for each eye using black cotton.

The nose is placed on rounds 35 and 36. Embroider a Y-shape with 2 pieces of brown cotton.

Fasten off the cotton per colour and weave in ends.

⇢⇢ 6. THE EARS ⇠⇠

Rnd 1: in 1 magic ring, 6 sc. Pull ring closed.

Rnd 2: *1 sc, 1 inc * x 3 = 9 sts.

Rnd 3: *2 sc, 1 inc * x 3 = 12 sts.

Rnd 4: *3 sc, 1 inc * x 3 = 15 sts.

Rnd 5: 15 sc.

Rnd 6: *4 sc, 1 inc * x 3 = 18 sts.

Rnd 7 to 14: 18 sc (8 rnds).

Rnd 15: *4 sc, 1 dec* x 3 = 15 sts.

Rnd 16 and 17: 15 sc (2 rnds).

Rnd 18: *3 sc, 1 dec* x 3 = 12 sts.

Rnd 19: 12 sc. Finish with 1 sl st into the 1st st.

Fasten off, leaving a 25 cm tail. Finish with an invisible finish.

Flatten the ears and fold the base in two to join the edges by stitching. Pin them to the top of the head and stitch them on tightly.

Fasten off and weave in ends.

BASIL
THE BOUNCY BEAR

Basil is a real gymnast! He climbs trees, rolls over, jumps over streams
by balancing on logs and climbs rocks... His days are pretty busy.
Roll on tomorrow for more bouncing adventures!

YOU WILL NEED:

1 x 2.5 mm crochet hook
Krea Deluxe organic cotton yarn
• 25 g or 83 m Cognac 52
• 60 cm Black 28
Polyester wadding

METHOD

⇢ All pieces are crocheted in a spiral from a magic ring.

⇢ You will first crochet the arms and the first leg to
be joined to the body when complete. The second
leg, body and head are then crocheted without
fastening off.

⇢ The muzzle and ears are crocheted last.

⇥ 1. THE ARMS ⇤

You should crochet the arms without stuffing them. Make 2.

Rnd 1: 6 sc into a magic ring. Pull ring closed.

Rnd 2: 6 inc= 12 sts.

Rnd 3 to 14: 12 sc (12 rnds)

Rnd 15: *1 dec, 4 sc* x 2 = 10 sts

Rnd 16: close the opening of the arm with 4 sc

Fasten off, leaving a 15 cm tail. Weave in ends. Place the arms to one side.

⇥ 2. THE LEGS ⇤

1ST LEG:

Rnd 1: 6 sc into a magic ring. Pull ring closed.

Rnd 2: 6 inc = 12 sts.

Rnd 3: *1 sc, 1 inc* x 6 = 18 sts.

Rnd 4 (BLO): 18 sc.

Rnd 5 to 8: 18 sc (4 rnds).

Finish with 1 sl st. Fasten off, leaving a 20 cm tail for finishing. Place to one side.

2ND LEG:

Repeat the same steps as the 1st leg, but stop after round 8: do not crochet a slip stitch nor cut the yarn.

⇥ 3. THE BODY ⇤

You can now begin the body by joining the legs.

Rnd 9: 10 sc (front of the 2nd leg), 2 ch without tightening (= crotch), 18 sc (in the 1st leg), 2 sc (in only 1 loop of the 2 ch), 8 dc (back of the 2nd leg) = 40 sts.

Now the stitch marker should be on the side of the body.

Rnd 10: 10 sc, 2 sl st (in the other loop of the 2 ch), 28 sc = 40 sts.

Rnd 11: 10 sc, 2 inc 18 sc 2 inc 8 sc = 44 sts.

After the next round, use the yarn tail left from the 1st leg to hide any holes in the crotch. You can then stuff the legs. The body and head can be stuffed as you work or at the end, as you prefer.

Rnd 12 to 25: 44 sc (14 rnds).

Rnd 26: 1 sc, 1 dec, [*3 sc, 1 dec* x 8], 1 sc = 35 sts.

Rnd 27: 35 sc.

Rnd 28: *3 sc, 1 dec* x 7 = 28 sts.

Rnd 29: 28 sc.

Rnd 30: *5 sc, 1 dec* x 4 = 24 sts.

You are now up to the back of the bear. On the next round, you will crochet the arms to the body.

Rnd 31: 1 dec, 4 sc to attach first arm (for each sc, insert the hook in 1 st on the arm and 1 st on the body = 4 loops), 4 dec, 4 sc with the second arm (worked same as first arm), 3 dec = 16 sts.

⇤ Depending on how you crochet, the arms may appear a little off-centre. If so, you need to change their position, while keeping an identical number of stitches.

Rnd 32: 14 inc, 2 sc = 30 sts.

Finish stuffing the body. Do not fasten off.

⇥ 4. THE HEAD ⇤

Rnd 33: 2 sc, 1 inc, [*4 sc, 1 inc* x 5], 2 sc = 36 sts.

Rnd 34: *5 sc, 1 inc* x 6 = 42 sts.

Rnd 35: 3 sc, 1 inc, [*6 sc, 1 inc* x 5], 3 sc = 48 sts.

Rnd 36 to 43: 48 sc (8 rnds).

Rnd 44: 2 sc, 1 dec, [*6 sc, 1 dec* x 5], 4 sc = 42 sts.

Rnd 45: *5 sc, 1 dec * x 6 = 36 sts.

Rnd 46: 3 sc, 1 dec, [*4 sc, 1 dec* x 5], 1 sc = 30 sts.

Rnd 47: 1 sc, 1 dec, [*3 sc, 1 dec* x 5], 2 sc = 24 sts.

Rnd 48: *2 sc, 1 dec* x 6 = 18 sts.

Rnd 49: *1 sc, 1 dec* x 4 = 12 sts.

Finish stuffing the head.

Rnd 50: 6 dec = 6 sts.

Fasten off, leaving a 20 cm tail. Finish with an invisible finish and weave in ends.

⤜ 5. THE NOSE ⤛

Rnd 1: 6 sc into a magic ring. Pull ring closed.

Rnd 2: 6 inc = 12 sts.

Rnd 3 (BLO): 12 sc.

Rnd 4: 12 sc.

Rnd 5: 12 inc = 24 sts.

Finish with 1 sl st. Fasten off, leaving a 30 cm tail. Finish with an invisible finish.

Pin the nose to the head between rounds 33 and 40, making sure it is central and in line with the neck.

Stitch it on while filling it a little before the final stitch.

Fasten off, and weave in ends.

⤜ 6. THE EARS ⤛

Rnd 1: 6 sc into a magic ring. Pull ring closed.

Rnd 2: 6 inc = 12 sts.

Rnd 3: *2 sc, 1 inc* x 4 = 16 sts.

Rnd 4 and 5: 16 sc (2 rnds).

Finish with 1 sl st. Fasten off, leaving a 30 cm tail. Finish with an invisible finish.

Flatten the ears and pin them to the side of the head while bending them forwards slightly, with the base being positioned at round 42 and the top between rounds 48 and 49. Stitch them tightly. Fasten off and weave in ends.

⤛ Crocheting in a spiral can lead to a slightly offset finish, with the rounds not being perfectly in line. So, I slightly change the position of the 2nd ear.

⤜ 7. THE EYES AND SNOUT ⤛

The eyes are placed on a stitch on round 40 and are separated by 6 stitches. Embroider 3 vertical points in black for each eye.

The snout is made up of 4 fanned out points, with the tip towards the bottom, on rounds 2 and 3 of the nose, and 1 vertical point which covers round 1 of the nose.

Fasten off and weave in ends.

HERMIONE
❧ THE WISE LIONESS ❧

Hermione lives across a large territory owned by her father.
One day, she will take over the duty of protecting and ensuring harmony
in her kingdom. She is well aware of her sense of duty! In the meantime,
she is observing, listening and contemplating...

YOU WILL NEED:

1 x 2.25 mm crochet hook
Krea Deluxe organic cotton yarn:
• 19 g or 63 m Croissant 53
• 1 m Black 28
Polyester wadding

METHOD

⇢ All of our pieces are crocheted in a spiral using a
magic ring.

⇢ Begin by crocheting the arms and the first leg before
joining these to the body when ready. The second
leg, the body and the head are then crotcheted
without fastening off.

⇢ The ears are then crocheted last.

⇶ 1. THE ARMS ⇇

You should crochet the arms without stuffing them. Make 2.

Rnd 1: 6 sc into a magic ring. Pull ring closed.

Rnd 2: 6 inc = 12 sts.

Rnd 3 to 14: 12 sc (12 rnds).

Rnd 15: *1 dec, 4 sc* x 2 = 10 sts.

Rnd 16: close the opening on the arm with 4 sc. Fasten off, leaving a 15 cm tail. Weave in ends. Place the arms to one side.

⇶ 2. THE LEGS ⇇

1ST LEG:

Rnd 1: 5 sc into a magic ring. Pull ring closed.

Rnd 2: 5 inc = 10 sts.

Rnd 3: *1 sc, 1 inc* x 5 = 15 sts.

Rnd 4 to 9: 15 sc (6 rnds).

Finish with 1 sl st. Fasten off, leaving a 20 cm tail and leave to one side.

2ND LEG:

Repeat as the 1st leg, but stop after round 9: do not crochet the slip stitch, do not fasten off.

⇶ 3. THE BODY ⇇

You can now begin the body by joining the legs. Place a stitch marker in the 1st stitch.

Rnd 10: 9 sc (in the 2nd leg), 2 ch without tightening (= crotch), 15 sc (in the 1st leg), 2 sc (in only 1 loop of the 2 ch), 6 sc (in the 2nd leg) = 34 sts.

Now the stitch marker should be on the side of the body.

Rnd 11: 9 sc, 2 sc (in the other loop of the 2 ch), 23 sc = 34 sts.

After the next round, use the yarn tail left from the 1st leg to hide any holes in the crotch. You can then stuff the legs. The body and head can be stuffed as you work or at the end, as you prefer.

Rnd 12 to 26: 34 sc (15 rnds).

Rnd 27: [*7 sc, 1 dec* x 3], 5 sc, 1 dec = 30 sts.

Rnd 28: 2 sc, 1 dec, [*6 sc, 1 dec* x 3], 2 sc = 26 sts.

Rnd 29: 2 sc, 1 dec, 12 sc, 1 dec, 8 sc = 24 sts.

You are now at the back of the lioness. In the next round, you will crochet the arms to the body.

Rnd 30: 1 dec, 4 sc to attach an arm (for each sc, insert the hook in 1 st on the arm and 1 st on the body = 4 loops), 4 dec, 4 sc with the other arm (worked same as first arm), 3 dec. Leave last st unworked. = 17 sts.

Move the stitch marker to last stitch completed (= new starting point of the rounds), now crochet a 4th dec = 16 sts.

⇇ Depending on how you crochet, the arms may appear a little off-centre. If so, you need to change their position, while keeping an identical number of stitches.

Rnd 31: 13 inc, 2 sc, 1 inc = 30 sts.

Finish stuffing the body. Do not fasten off.

⇶ 4. THE HEAD ⇇

Rnd 32: 2 sc, 1 inc, [*4 sc, 1 inc* x 5], 2 sc = 36 sts.

Rnd 33: *5 sc, 1 inc* x 6 = 42 sts.

Rnd 34: 7 sc, 1 inc, 10 sc, 1 inc, 10 sc, 1 inc, 12 sc = 45 sts.

Rnd 35 to 40: 45 sc (6 rnds).

Rnd 41: 8 sc, 1 dec, 10 sc, 1 dec, 10 sc, 1 dec, 11 sc = 42 sts.

Rnd 42: *5 sc, 1 dec* x 6 = 36 sts.

Rnd 43: 2 sc, 1 dec, [*4 sc, 1 dec* x 5], 2 sc = 30 sts.

Rnd 44: *3 sc, 1 dec* x 6 = 24 sts.

Rnd 45: 1 sc, 1 dec, [*2 sc, 1 dec* x 5], 1 sc = 18 sts.

Rnd 46: *1 sc, 1 dec* x 4 = 12 sts.

Finish stuffing the head.

Rnd 47: 6 dec = 6 sts.

Fasten off, leaving a 20 cm tail. Finish with an invisible finish and weave in ends.

→» 5. THE FACE «←

USING BLACK YARN (4 STRANDS):

The nose should be in a Y-shape: make a horizontal line 2 stitches wide between rounds 35 and 36, and then a vertical line at the centre from round 35 to round 34. The vertical line should surround the horizontal line to curve downwards.

The eyes are placed between rounds 38 and 39 and spaced 4 or 5 stitches apart. Embroider 4 horizontal points 2 stitches wide for each eye.

Fasten off and weave in ends.

USING BLACK YARN (2 STRANDS):

The mouth is made up of a horizontal line 4 stitches wide between rounds 33 and 34. Insert the yarn beneath the vertical line forming the nose. Add a small diagonal line on each side.

In the inner corner of each eye, embroider a small downward vertical line.

Fasten off and weave in ends.

→» 6. THE EARS «←

Rnd 1: 6 sc into a magic ring. Pull ring closed.

Rnd 2: 6 inc = 12 sts.

Rnd 3: *2 sc, 1 inc* x 4 = 16 sts.

Rnd 4 to 6: 16 sc (3 rnds).

Finish with 1 sl st. Fasten off, leaving a 30 cm tail. Finish with an invisible finish.

Flatten the ears and pin them to the side of the head folding them slightly forward.

The base should be placed at round 39 and the top at round 44 (7 or 8 stitches separate the ears on this round). Stitch them tightly.

Fasten off and weave in ends.

«← I embroider the nose first as it is central to the neck. This makes it much easier to then position the eyes.

PINKY
✿ THE CLEVER PIG ✿

Pinky is hungry to learn, he reads a lot of books and is always watching a documentary. He is interested in everything and anything, including geography, the natural world, people, chemistry, and so on. He often helps his friends when they don't understand something. He is destined to become a teacher!

YOU WILL NEED:

1 x 2.5 mm crochet hook
Krea Deluxe organic cotton yarn
• 25 g or 83 m Warm Pink 10
• 50 cm Earth Brown 29
Polyester wadding

METHOD

⇒ All of our pieces are crocheted in a spiral using a magic ring (except the snout).

⇒ Start by crocheting the arms and the first leg to be joined to the body when ready. The second leg, body and head can then be crocheted without fastening off.

⇒ The snout and ears are crocheted last.

74

➻ 1. THE ARMS ➻

You should crochet the arms without stuffing them. Make 2.

Rnd 1: 6 sc into a magic ring. Pull ring closed.

Rnd 2: 6 inc = 12 sts.

Rnd 3 to 14: 12 sc (12 rnds).

Rnd 15: *1 dec, 4 sc* x 2 = 10 sts.

Rnd 16: close off the opening of the arm with 4 sc.

Fasten off, leaving a 15 cm tail. Weave in ends. Place the arms to one side.

➻ 2. THE LEGS ➻

1ST LEG:

Rnd 1: 6 sc into a magic ring. Pull ring closed.

Rnd 2: 6 inc = 12 sts.

Rnd 3: *1 sc, 1 inc* x 6 = 18 sts.

Rnd 4 to 8: 18 sc (5 rnds).

Finish off with a sl st. Fasten off, leaving a 20 cm tail and leave to one side.

2ND LEG:

Repeat as the 1st leg, but stop after round 8: do not crochet the slip stitch, do not fasten off.

➻ 3. THE BODY ➻

You can now begin the body by joining the legs. Place a stitch marker in the 1st stitch.

Rnd 9: 10 sc (front of the 2nd leg), 2 ch without tightening (= crotch), 18 sc (in the 1st leg), 2 sc (in only 1 loop of the 2 ch), 8 sc (back of the 2nd leg) = 40 sts.

Now the stitch marker should be on the side of the body.

Rnd 10: 10 sc, 2 sc (in the other loop of the 2 ch), 28 sc = 40 sts.

Rnd 11: 10 sc, 2 inc, 18 sc, 2 inc, 8 sc = 44 sts.

After the next round, use the yarn tail left from the 1st leg to hide any holes in the crotch. You can then stuff the legs. The body and head can be stuffed as you work or at the end, as you prefer.

Rnd 12 to 25: 44 sc (14 rnds).

Rnd 26: 1 sc, 1 dec, [*3 sc, 1 dec* x 8], 1 sc = 35 sts.

Rnd 27: 35 sc.

Rnd 28: *3 sc, 1 dec* x 7 = 28 sts.

Rnd 29: 28 sc.

Rnd 30: *5 sc, 1 dec* x 4 = 24 sts.

You are now on the pig's back. In the next round, you will crochet the arms to the body.

Rnd 31: 1 dec, 4 sc to attach an arm (for each sc, insert the hook in 1 st on the arm and 1 st on the body = 4 loops), 4 dec, 4 sc with the other arm (worked same as first arm), 3 dec = 16 sts.

➻ Depending on how you crochet, the arms may appear a little off-centre. If so, you need to change their position, while keeping an identical number of stitches.

Rnd 32: 14 inc, 2 sc = 30 sts.

Finish stuffing the body. Do not fasten off.

➻ 4. THE HEAD ➻

Rnd 33: 2 sc, 1 inc, [*4 sc, 1 inc* x 5], 2 sc = 36 sts.

Rnd 34: *5 sc, 1 inc * x 6 = 42 sts.

Rnd 35: 3 sc, 1 inc, [*6 sc, 1 inc* x 5], 3 sc = 48 sts.

Rnd 36 to 43: 48 sc (8 rnds).

Rnd 44: 2 sc, 1 dec, [*6 sc, 1 dec* x 5], 4 sc = 42 sts.

Rnd 45: *5 sc, 1 dec* x 6 = 36 sts.

Rnd 46: 3 sc, 1 dec [*4 sc, 1 dec* x 5], 1 sc = 30 sts.

Rnd 47: 1 sc, 1 dec, [*3 sc, 1 dec* x 5], 2 sc = 24 sts.

Rnd 48: *2 sc, 1 dec* x 6 = 18 sts.

Rnd 49: *1 sc 1 dec* x 4 = 12 sts.

Finish stuffing the head.

Rnd 50: 6 dec = 6 sts.

Fasten off, leaving a 20 cm tail. Finish with an invisible finish and weave in ends.

⇒ 5. THE SNOUT ⇐

5 ch.

Rnd 1: sc in 2nd ch from hook, 2 sc, 3 sc in the same stitch, then on the other side of the chain: 2 sc, 1 inc = 10 sts.

Rnd 2: 1 inc, 2 sc, 3 inc, 2 sc, 2 inc = 16 sts.

Rnd 3 (FLO): 16 sl st.

Fasten off, leaving a 30 cm tail for attaching. Finish with an invisible finish.

With two pins, place the snout on the head between rounds 34 and 39, ensuring it is central in line with the neck. Then stitch this using the rear loops on round 2.

Fasten off and weave in ends.

⇒ 6. THE EYES AND NOSTRILS ⇐

The eyes are positioned on a stitch on round 38 and separated by 9 or 10 stitches (the space between the snout and eyes should be even). Using the brown yarn, embroider 3 vertical points for each eye.

Each nostril is represented by 1 vertical point inside the snout.

Fasten off and weave in ends.

⇒ 7. THE EARS ⇐

Rnd 1: 6 sc into a magic ring. Pull ring closed.

Rnd 2: *1 sc, 1 inc* x 3 = 9 sts.

Rnd 3: *2 sc, 1 inc* x 3 = 12 sts.

Rnd 4: *3 sc, 1 inc* x 3 = 15 sts.

Rnd 5 and 6: 15 sc (2 rnds).

Rnd 7: *3 sc, 1 dec* x 3 = 12 sts.

Rnd 8: 12 sc, 1 sl st.

Fasten off, leaving a 30 cm tail for attaching. Finish with an invisible finish.

Flatten the ears and pin them at an angle and flat, with the base of the ears towards the bottom on round 45 and the top at round 48 (5 stitches separate the ears on this round).

Stitch them tight at the base, while closing the opening (do not go all the way around the ears, they need to stay flat).

Fasten off and weave in ends.

ADRIENNE
THE MUSICAL ELEPHANT

For Adrienne, music is life! A touch of jazz never fails to bring a smile...
With her trunk, she loves to play a few notes. One day she will be
a famous musician and invited to the most prestigious concerts.

YOU WILL NEED:

1 x 2.5 mm crochet hook
Krea Deluxe organic cotton yarn:
• 27 g or 90 m Grey 49
• 50 cm Black 28
Polyester wadding

METHOD

→→ All pieces are crocheted in a spiral using a magic ring.

→→ You can start with the arms, trunk, ears and the
first leg to be joined to the body and head when
needed. The second leg, body and head can then be
crocheted without fastening off.

→→ When attaching, you should only crochet the base of
the trunk.

⇢ 1. THE ARMS ⇠

You should crochet the arms without stuffing them. Make 2.

Rnd 1: 5 sc into a magic ring. Pull ring closed.

Rnd 2: 5 inc = 10 sts.

Rnd 3: *1 sc, 1 inc* x 5 = 15 sts.

Rnd 4 (BLO): 15 sc.

Rnd 5 to 11: 15 sc (7 rnds).

Stuff the bottoms of the arms only very lightly.

Rnd 12: *3 sc, 1 dec* x 3 = 12 sts.

Rnd 13 and 14: 12 sc (2 rnds).

Rnd 15: *4 sc, 1 dec* x 2 = 10 sts.

Rnd 16: close off the opening of the arm with 4 ch.

Fasten off, leaving a 15 cm tail. Weave in ends. Place the arms to one side.

⇢ 2. THE TRUNK ⇠

Rnd 1: 5 sc into a magic ring. Pull ring closed.

Rnd 2: 5 inc = 10 sts.

Rnd 3 (BLO): 10 sc.

Do not forget to put the piece the right way up (with the V- or X-stitches on the outside).

Rnd 4 to 7: 10 sc (4 rnds).

Rnd 8: 2 sc, 1 inc, 7 sc = 11 sts.

Rnd 9: 3 sc, 1 inc, 7 sc = 12 sts.

Fill the trunk partially, as it should remain flexible.

Rnd 10: 12 sc.

Rnd 11: 3 sc, 1 inc, 8 sc = 13 sts.

Rnd 12: 13 sc.

Rnd 13: 2 sc, 1 inc, 3 sc, 1 inc, 6 sc = 15 sts.

Rnd 14: 6 sc, 1 inc, 8 sc = 16 sts.

Rnd 15: 16 sc, 1 sl st.

Fasten off, leaving a 20 cm tail for attaching. Leave to one side.

⇢ 3. THE EARS ⇠

Make 2.

Rnd 1: 6 sc into a magic ring. Pull ring closed.

Rnd 2: 6 inc = 12 sts.

Rnd 3: *1 sc, 1 inc* x 6 = 18 sts.

Rnd 4: *2 sc, 1 inc* x 6 = 24 sts.

Rnd 5: *3 sc, 1 inc* x 6 = 30 sts.

Rnd 6: *4 sc, 1 inc* x 6 = 36 sts.

The ears should form a hexagon (6 sides with 6 stitches each). Fold the first worked side in half and work 3 sc working through both sides (4 loops on your hook). You will join the ear to the head using these stitches.

Fasten off, leaving a 15 cm tail. Weave in end.

⇢ 4. THE LEGS ⇠

1ST LEG:

Rnd 1: 6 sc into a magic ring. Pull ring closed.

Rnd 2: 6 inc = 12 sts.

Rnd 3: *1 sc, 1 inc* x 6 = 18 sts.

Rnd 4 (BLO): 18 sc.

Rnd 5 to 8: 18 sc (4 rnds).

Finish off with a sl st. Fasten off, leaving a 20 cm tail and leave to one side.

2ND LEG:

Repeat as the 1st leg, but stop after round 8: do not crochet the slip stitch, do not fasten off.

⇒⇒ 5. THE BODY ⇐⇐

You can now begin the body by joining the legs. Place a stitch marker in the 1st stitch.

Rnd 9: 10 sc (front of 2nd leg), 2 ch without tightening (= crotch), 18 sc (on the 1st leg), 2 sc (in only 1 loop of the 2 ch), 8 sc (back of 2nd leg) = 40 sts.

Now the stitch marker should be on the side of the body.

Rnd 10: 10 sc, 2 sc (in the other loop on the 2 ch), 28 sc = 40 sts.

Rnd 11: 10 sc, 2 inc, 18 sc, 2 inc, 8 sc = 44 sts.

After the next round, use the yarn tail left from the 1st leg to hide any holes in the crotch. You can then stuff the legs. The body and head can be stuffed as you work or at the end as you prefer.

Rnd 12 and 13: 44 sc (2 rnds).

Rnd 14: 2 sc, 1 inc, 20 sc, 1 inc, 20 sc = 46 sts.

Rnd 15 to 26: 46 sc (12 rnds).

Rnd 27: 3 sc, 1 dec, 22 sc, 1 dec, 17 sc = 44 sts.

Rnd 28: 44 sc.

Rnd 29: 1 sc, 1 dec, [*3 sc, 1 dec* x 8], 1 sc = 35 sts.

Rnd 30: 35 sc.

Rnd 31: *3 sc, 1 dec* x 7 = 28 sts.

Rnd 32: 28 sc.

Rnd 33: *5 sc, 1 dec* x 4 = 24 sts.

You are now on the elephant's back. On the next round, you can crochet the arms to the body.

Rnd 34: 2 sc, 4 sc with one arm (for each sc, insert the hook in 1 st on the arm and 1 st on the body = 4 loops), 8 sc, 4 sc with the other arm (= 4 loops), 6 sc = 24 sts.

⇐⇐ Depending on how you crochet, the arms may appear a little off-centre. If so, you need to change their position, while keeping an identical number of stitches.

Rnd 35: *3 sc, 1 inc* x 6 = 30 sts.

Finish stuffing the body. Do not fasten off.

⇒⇒ 6. THE HEAD ⇐⇐

Rnd 36: 2 sc, 1 inc [*4 sc, 1 inc* x 5] 2 sc = 36 sts.

Rnd 37: *5 sc, 1 inc* x 6 = 42 sts.

Rnd 38: 3 sc, 1 inc [*6 sc, 1 inc* x 5] 3 sc = 48 sts.

Rnd 39 to 41: 48 sc (3 rnds).

⇐⇐ The trunk and ears will be crocheted to the head at rounds 42 and 49. Depending on how you crochet, they may appear a little off-centre. If so, you need to change their position, while respecting the total number of stitches.

On the next round, you will crochet the trunk to the head.

Rnd 49: 5 sc, 1 dec, 2 sc, 3 sc (for each sc, insert the crochet in 1 st on the ear and 1 st on the head = 4 loops), 1 dec, [*5 sc, 1 dec* x 2], 3 sc (for each sc, insert the crochet hook in 1 st on the ear and 1 st on the head = 4 loops), 2 sc, 1 dec, 5 sc, 1 dec = 36 sts.

Rnd 50: 2 sc, 1 dec, [*4 sc, 1 dec* x 5], 2 sc = 30 sts.

Rnd 51: 1 sc, 1 dec, [*3 sc, 1 dec* x 5], 2 sc = 24 sts.

Rnd 52: *2 sc, 1 dec* x 6 = 18 sts.

Rnd 53: *1 sc, 1 dec* x 4 = 12 sts.

Finish stuffing the head.

Rnd 54: 6 dec = 6 sts.

Fasten off, leaving a 20 cm tail. Finish with an invisible finish and weave in ends.

⤏ 7. THE EYES AND PUPILS ⬿

The eyes should be positioned on a stitch at round 43 and are separated by 9 stitches (either 2 or 3 stitches from the trunk). Using the black yarn, embroider 3 vertical points.

The pupils are made using 3 diagonal points 1.5 stitches wide, just on top of the eyes. Embroider them using the grey yarn.

Fasten off and weave in ends.

Rnd 42: 19 sc (in the stitches on the head), 10 sc (only in the stitches on the trunk from the stitch next to the sl st), skip 5 stitches (on the head), 24 sc (in the stitches on the head) = 53 sts.

Rnd 43: 19 sc, 1 dec, 6 sc, 1 dec, 24 sc = 51 sts.

Rnd 44: 20 sc, 3 dec, 25 sc = 48 sts.

Rnd 45 to 47: 48 sc (3 rnds).

Using the yarn placed to one side, stitch the top of the trunk with the 5 skipped sts to stop the stuffing from coming out.

Rnd 48: 3 sc, 1 dec, [*6 sc, 1 dec* x 5] 3 sc = 42 sts.

On the next round, you will crochet the ears to the head. Position them facing the front. They should be crocheted on the last 3 stitches of the ears.

HORACE
✦ THE HUNGRY HIPPO ✦

Horace loves to spend his days in the water snuggling up to his mum
or lazing around on his back. Both of them yawn and sleep awaiting the sunset...
Once night falls, Horace comes out of the water and tucks into
his favourite dinner of buffalo grass.

YOU WILL NEED:

1 x 2.5 mm crochet hook
Krea Deluxe organic cotton yarn:
• 27 g or 90 m Brown 30
• 50 cm Black 28
Polyester wadding

METHOD

⇶ All of the pieces are crocheted in a spiral using a
magic ring (except the snout).

⇶ You should begin by crocheting the arms and the
first leg to be joined to the body when ready. The
second leg, body and head can then be crocheted
without fastening off.

⇶ The snout and ears are crocheted last.

➺ 1. THE ARMS ⭇

You should crochet the arms without stuffing them. Make 2.

Rnd 1: 6 sc into a magic ring. Pull ring closed.

Rnd 2: 6 inc = 12 sts.

Rnd 3 (BLO): 12 sc.

Rnd 4 to 14: 12 sc (11 rnds).

Rnd 15: *1 dec, 4 sc* x 2 = 10 sts.

Rnd 16: close off the opening of the arm with 4 sc.

Cut the yarn at 15 cm, draw it through the loop and insert. Place the arms to one side.

➺ 2. THE LEGS ⭇

1ST LEG:

Rnd 1: 6 sc into a magic ring. Pull ring closed.

Rnd 2: 6 inc = 12 sts.

Rnd 3: *1 sc, 1 inc* x 6 = 18 sts.

Rnd 4 (BLO): 18 sc.

Rnd 5 to 8: 18 sc (4 rnds).

Finish off with a sl st. Fasten off, leaving a 20 cm tail and leave to one side.

2ND LEG:

Repeat as the 1st leg, but stop after round 8: do not crochet the slip stitch, do not fasten off.

➺ 3. THE BODY ⭇

You can now begin the body by joining the legs. Place a stitch marker in the 1st stitch.

Rnd 9: 10 sc (front of the 2nd leg), 2 ch without tightening (= crotch), 18 sc (in the 1st leg), 2 sc (in only 1 of the 2 ch), 8 sc (back of the 2nd leg) = 40 sts.

Now the stitch marker should be on the side of the body.

Rnd 10: 10 sc, 2 sc (in the other loop of the 2 ch), 28 sc = 40 sts.

Rnd 11: 10 sc, 2 inc, 18 sc, 2 inc, 8 sc = 44 sts.

After the next round, use the yarn tail left from the 1st leg to hide any holes in the crotch. You can then stuff the legs. The body and head can be stuffed as you work or at the end, as you prefer.

Rnd 12 and 13: 44 sc (2 rnds).

Rnd 14: 2 sc, 1 inc, 20 sc, 1 inc, 20 sc = 46 sts.

Rnd 15 to 26: 46 sc (12 rnds).

Rnd 27: 3 sc, 1 dec, 22 sc, 1 dec, 17 sc = 44 sts.

Rnd 28: 44 sc.

Rnd 29: 1 sc, 1 dec, [*3 sc, 1 dec* x 8], 1 sc = 35 sts.

Rnd 30: 35 sc.

Rnd 31: *3 sc, 1 dec* x 7 = 28 sts.

Rnd 32: 28 sc.

Rnd 33: *5 sc, 1 dec* x 4 = 24 sts.

You are now on the hippo's back. On the next round, you can crochet the arms to the body.

Rnd 34: 2 sc, 4 sc with first arm for each sc, insert the hook in 1 st on the arm and 1 st on the body = 4 loops), 8 sc, 4 sc with the second arm (worked same as first arm), 6 sc = 24 sts.

⭇ Depending on how you crochet, the arms may appear a little off-centre. If so, you need to change their position, while keeping an identical number of stitches.

Rnd 35: *3 sc, 1 inc* x 6 = 30 sts.

Finish stuffing the body. Do not fasten off.

⇝ 4. THE HEAD ⇜

Rnd 36: 2 sc, 1 inc, [*4 sc, 1 inc* x 5], 2 sc = 36 sts.

Rnd 37: *5 sc, 1 inc* x 6 = 42 sts.

Rnd 38: 3 sc, 1 inc, [*6 sc, 1 inc* x 5], 3 sc = 48 sts

Rnd 39 to 47: 48 sc (9 rnds).

Rnd 48: 3 sc, 1 dec, [*6 sc, 1 dec* x 5], 3 dc = 42 sts.

Rnd 49: *5 sc, 1 dec* x 6 = 36 sts.

Rnd 50: 2 sc, 1 dec, [*4 sc, 1 dec* x 5], 2 sc = 30 sts.

Rnd 51: 1 sc, 1 dec, [*3 sc, 1 dec* x 5], 2 sc = 24 sts.

Rnd 52: *2 sc, 1 dec* x 6 = 18 sts.

Rnd 53: *1 sc, 1 dec* x 4 = 12 sts.

Finish stuffing the head.

Rnd 54: 6 dec = 6 sts.

Fasten off, leaving a 20 cm tail. Finish with an invisible finish and weave in ends.

⇝ 5. THE SNOUT ⇜

You can now crochet in a spiral from a chain. To help you, on the following page is a diagram showing rounds 1 to 5.

10 ch.

Rnd 1: 1 inc in 2nd ch from hook, 7 sc, 3 sc in the same ch, turn and work other side of ch, 8 sc = 20 sts

Rnd 2: 2 inc, 7 sc, 3 inc, 7 sc, 1 inc = 26 sts.

Rnd 3: 1 inc, 1 sc, 1 inc, 10 sc, 1 inc, 1 sc, 1 inc, 10 sc = 30 sts.

Rnd 4: 1 inc, 3 sc, 1 inc, 10 sc, 1 inc, 3 sc, 1 inc, 10 sc = 34 sts.

Rnd 5: 1 inc, 6 sc, 1 inc, 8 sc, 1 inc, 6 sc, 1 inc, 10 sc = 38 sts.

Rnd 6 to 9: 38 sc (4 rnds).

Finish off with 1 sl st. Fasten off, leaving a 35 cm tail. Close off with an invisible finish and weave in end.

Begin to stuff the snout, then pin it to the head covering rounds 35 (= the neck) to 45. Stitch this while retaining the oval shape. Finish by stuffing it before closing off your stitching.

Fasten off and weave in ends.

⇜ I often insert pins all the way around the snout to hold it in place during stitching.

DIAGRAM OF THE SNOUT

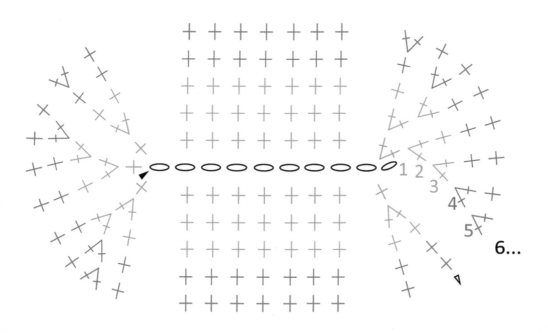

⇢⇢ 6. THE EYES AND NOSTRILS ⇠⇠

The eyes are placed on a stitch at round 48 and separated by 7 stitches. Embroider 3 vertical points in black for each eye. Do not cut the yarn before moving on to the nostrils.

Each nostril is placed on a stitch at round 5 of the snout, formed by 3 vertical points.

These are separated by 3 stitches.

Fasten off and weave in ends.

⇢⇢ 7. THE EARS ⇠⇠

Take care to leave at least 15 cm of yarn at the end of the magic ring to use when fastening.

Rnd 1: 6 sc into a magic ring. Pull ring closed.

Fasten off leaving a 20 cm tail for attaching.

Pin the ears to the top of the head (round 51). Each should be positioned along an imaginary line formed by one of the nostrils and an eye. Stitch them tightly.

Fasten off and weave in ends.

MILLIE AND TILLY ARE ABOUT 12 CM TALL

MILLIE AND TILLY

THE SHY TORTOISES

Despite their hardy shells, Millie and Tilly are not very confident and often take refuge inside when things get stressful. Fortunately, their friends bring them out of their shells and nurture their kind-hearted nature.

YOU WILL NEED:

1 x 2.25 mm crochet hook
Polyester wadding
Krea Deluxe organic cotton yarn:
• 60 cm Black 28 (face)
Millie: • 14 g or 47 m Cream 02 (yarn A, body)
• 10 g or 33 m Khaki Green 39 (yarn B, shell)
Tilly: • 14 g or 47 m Linen 46 (yarn A, body)
• 10 g or 33 m Cognac 52 (yarn B, shell)

METHOD

➻➤ All of the pieces are crocheted in a spiral from a magic ring.

➻➤ Begin by crocheting the tail, 4 legs and body (stomach and then the back).

➻➤ The head and shell should be crocheted last.

➻➤ Partially stuff your creation if you want the tortoise to be able to move in and out of its shell.

TILLY

MILLIE

⇢ 1. THE TAIL ⇠

You should crochet the tail without stuffing it.

With yarn A:

Rnd 1: 6 sc into a magic ring. Pull ring closed.

Rnd 2: *1 sc, 1 inc* x 3 = 9 sts.

Rnd 3 to 5: 9 sc (3 rnds).

Rnd 6: close off the opening of the tail with 4 sc.

Fasten off, leaving a 15 cm tail. Weave in ends. Place the tail to one side.

⇢ 2. THE FEET ⇠

Make 4.

With yarn A:

Rnd 1: 6 sc into a magic ring. Pull ring closed.

Rnd 2: 6 inc = 12 sts.

Rnd 3 (BLO): *3 sc, 1 inc* x 3 = 15 sts.

Rnd 4: 15 sc.

Rnd 5: *3 sc, 1 dec* x 3 = 12 sts.

Rnd 6 to 10: 12 sc (5 rnds).

Partially stuff.

Rnd 11: close off the opening of the foot with 5 sc.

Fasten off, leaving a 15 cm tail. Weave in ends. Place feet to one side.

⇢ 3. THE BODY ⇠

With yarn A, start by crocheting the stomach:

Rnd 1: 6 sc into a magic ring. Pull ring closed.

Rnd 2: 6 inc = 12 sts.

Rnd 3: *1 sc, 1 inc* x 6 = 18 sts.

Rnd 4: 1 sc, 1 inc, [*2 sc, 1 inc* x 5] 1 sc = 24 sts.

Rnd 5: *3 sc, 1 inc* x 6 = 30 sts.

Rnd 6: 2 sc, 1 inc, [*4 sc, 1 inc* x 5], 2 sc = 36 sts.

Rnd 7: *5 sc, 1 inc* x 6 = 42 sts.

Rnd 8: 3 sc, 1 inc, [*6 sc, 1 inc* x 5], 3 sc = 48 sts.

Rnd 9: *7 sc, 1 inc* x 6 = 54 sts.

On the next round you will crochet the tail and feet to the body. Place the feet so as to hide the visible loops on round 3 on the least visible side (towards the stomach).

Rnd 10: 1 sc, 4 sc with the tail (insert the hook in 1 st on the arm and 1 st on the body = 4 loops), 2 sc, 5 sc with first foot (work as tail), 7 sc, 5 sc with second foot (work as tail), 12 sc, 5 sc with third foot (work as tail), 7 sc, 5 sc with last foot (work as tail), 1 sc = 54 sts.

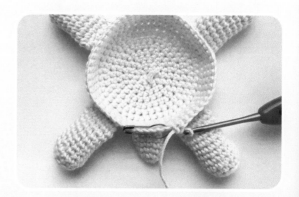

⇝ 4. THE HEAD ⇜

With yarn A:

Rnd 1: 6 sc into a magic ring. Pull ring closed.

Rnd 2: 6 inc = 12 sts.

Rnd 3: *1 sc, 1 inc* x 6 = 18 sts.

Rnd 4: *5 sc, 1 inc* x 3 = 21 sts.

Rnd 5 to 9: 21 sc (5 rnds).

Rnd 10: 4 dec, 13 sc = 17 sts. Place a marker in the 1st decrease st to mark throat.

Rnd 11: 10 sc, 1 dec, 5 sc = 16 sts.

Rnd 12 to 16: 16 sc (5 rnds).

Finish with 1 sl st. Fasten off, leaving a 30 cm tail. Close off with an invisible finish and weave in end.

Rnd 11 and 12: 54 sc (2 rnds).

Finish off with the back.

Rnd 13: *7 sc, 1 dec* x 6 = 48 sts.

Rnd 14: 3 sc, 1 dec, [*6 sc, 1 dec* x 5], 3 sc = 42 sts.

Rnd 15: *5 sc, 1 dec* x 6 = 36 sts.

Rnd 16: 36 sc.

Rnd 17: 2 sc, 1 dec, [*4 sc, 1 dec* x 5], 2 sc = 30 sts.

Rnd 18: *3 sc, 1 dec* x 6 = 24 sts.

Partially stuff to be able to insert the tortoise in its shell.

Rnd 19: 1 sc, 1 dec, [*2 sc, 1 dec* x 5], 1 sc = 18 sts.

Rnd 20: *1 sc, 1 dec* x 6 = 12 sts.

Finish stuffing the body.

Rnd 21: 6 dec = 6 sts.

Fasten off, leaving a 20 cm tail. Finish with an invisible finish and weave in ends.

The 4 decrease stitches on round 10 represent the throat. The head should be placed with the throat at the base.

Pin the head to the top of the back, with the base of the neck located between rounds 12 and 13 on the body and the neck on round 17. Stitch tightly and finish stuffing the neck before fastening off your last stitch.

⟶ 5. THE EYES AND MOUTH ⟵

The eyes are located on round 4 of the head, above the magic ring, and are spaced 7 stitches apart. For each eye, stitch 2 points on top of each other using the black yarn (4 strands).

The mouth is located between rounds 2 and 3 of the other side of the magic ring. Embroider 3 small points on the back using the black yarn (2 strands).

Fasten off and weave in ends.

⟶ 6. THE SHELL ⟵

THE UNDERSIDE:

With yarn B:

Rnd 1: 6 sc into a magic ring. Pull ring closed.

Rnd 2: 6 inc = 12 sts.

Rnd 3: *1 sc, 1 inc* x 6 = 18 sts.

Rnd 4: 1 sc, 1 inc, [*2 sc, 1 inc* x 5], 1 sc = 24 sts.

Rnd 5: *3 sc, 1 inc* x 6 = 30 sts.

Rnd 6: 2 sc, 1 inc, [*4 sc, 1 inc* x 5], 2 sc = 36 sts.

Rnd 7: *5 sc, 1 inc* x 2 = 42 sts.

Rnd 8: 3 sc, 1 inc, [*6 sc, 1 inc* x 5], 3 sc = 48 sts.

Rnd 9: *7 sc, 1 inc* x 6 = 54 sts.

On the next 2 rounds, make 2 folds which will be used for the front legs.

Rnd 10: 8 sc, 1 inc, 8 ch skip 8 sts., 1 inc, 8 sc, 1 inc, 8 ch skip 8 sts, 1 inc, [*8 sc, 1 inc* x 2] = 60 sts.

Rnd 11: 9 sc, 1 inc, 8 sc (in the chain), 1 sc (place a marker at this stitch, it will be crocheted first when joining the shell), 1 inc, 9 sc, 1 inc, 8 sc (in the chain), 1 sc, 1 inc, *9 sc, 1 inc* x 2 = 66 sts.

Finish off with 1 sl st.

⟵ The stitches on the perimeter between the two folds are where the head will be positioned.

Fasten off, leaving a 15 cm tail. Close off with an invisible finish and weave in end.

THE TOP:

With yarn B, crochet without any overedge on the increases to form a hexagon.

Rnd 1: 6 sc into a magic ring. Pull ring closed.

Rnd 2: 6 inc = 12 sts.

Rnd 3 (BLO): *1 sc, 1 inc* x 6 = 18 sts.

JOINING TOGETHER:

Place the top of the shell onto the underside (it is larger, this is normal), back against back, lining up both of the stitch markers.

← The next part is a little more complicated, but you will see it is easier than you think provided you keep your concentration.

Crochet 15 sc top and bottom together (for each sc, insert the crochet hook in 1 st on top and 1 st on the bottom = 4 loops on hook) 8 sc (in top shell only = location of the back leg), 1 sc top and bottom together (4 loops on hook) 6 sc (in top shell only = location of the tail), 1 sc top and bottom together (4 loops on hook) 8 sc (in top shell only = location of the other back leg) 10 sc top and together bottom (4 loops on hook).

← If you have over-stuffed the tortoise, now place it in its shell, with its back legs and tail in the folds between the top and underside, with the front legs in the folds on the underside. It would be a little too difficult to do this after joining the shell.

To finish joining together: 5 sc on the underside (for each sc, insert the crochet hook in 1 st on the top and 1 st on the underside = 4 loops on hook).

Finish off, with 1 sl st on the top of the shell.

Fasten off leaving a 15 cm tail. Close off with an invisible finish and weave in end.

Rnd 4: *2 dc, 1 inc* x 6 = 24 sts.

Rnd 5 (BLO): *3 dc 1 inc* x 6 = 30 sts.

Rnd 6: *4 dc, 1 inc* x 6 = 36 sts.

Rnd 7 (BLO): *5 dc 1 inc* x 6 = 42 sts.

Rnd 8: *6 dc, 1 inc* x 6 = 48 sts.

Rnd 9 (BLO): *7 dc 1 inc* x 6 = 54 sts.

Rnd 10: *8 dc 1 inc* x 6 = 60 sts.

Rnd 11 (BLO): *9 dc 1 inc* x 6 = 66 sts.

On the next round, stop before the end of the round.

Rnd 12: [*10 sc, 1 inc* x 5], 2 sc = 62 sts. Leave last 9 sts unworked.

Move the stitch marker to the next (63rd) stitch.

BAZ AND GAZ
THE CHIRPY BIRDS

From sunrise each day, Baz and Gaz sing their happy tune!
Their good humour enchants the surrounding countryside.

YOU WILL NEED:

1 x 2.25 mm crochet hook
Krea Deluxe organic cotton yarn:
Gaz: • 9 g or 30 m Croissant 53 (yarn A, body)
Baz: • 9 g or 30 m Cognac 52 (yarn A, body)
• 60 cm Earth Brown 29 (yarn B, beak)
• 40 cm Black 28 (eyes)
Katia cotton yarn: 3 g or 10 m of Oceania 63 (yarn C, wings and tail)
Polyester wadding

METHOD

→→ All of the pieces are crocheted in a spiral using a magic ring (except the beak and tail).

→→ Begin by creating the wings to join to the body when needed. The body and head can be crocheted without fastening off.

→→ You can crochet the beak (in rows) and tail (in a spiral around a chain) last.

→→ Partially fill to be able to mould the shape of the bird: the base of the stomach flat and head pointing forwards.

BAZ

GAZ

⇛ I. THE WINGS ⇚

Make 2.

With yarn C:

Rnd 1: 6 sc into a magic ring. Pull ring closed.

Rnd 2: 6 inc = 12 sts.

Rnd 3: *1 sc, 1 inc* x 6 = 18 sts.

Rnd 4: *2 sc, 1 inc* x 6 = 24 sts.

Rnd 5: *3 sc, 1 inc* x 6 = 30 sts.

Fold the wing in half with the wrong sides facing with last st at one of the corners of the semi-circle formed. Crochet around the circular edge through both sides of the wing (= 4 loops on hook).

Then crochet 1 ch, turn and crochet 4 sc (you will need to crochet in these last 4 stitches when joining to the body).

Fasten off, leaving a 15 cm tail. Weave in end. Place the wings to one side.

⇛ 2. THE BODY AND HEAD ⇚

THE BODY:

Stuff as you go or before you finish, as you prefer.

With yarn A:

Rnd 1: 6 sc into a magic ring. Pull ring closed.

Rnd 2: 6 inc = 12 sts.

Rnd 3: *1 sc, 1 inc* x 6 = 18 sts.

Rnd 4: 1 sc, 1 inc, [*2 sc, 1 inc* x 5], 1 sc = 24 sts.

Rnd 5: *3 sc, 1 inc* x 6 = 30 sts.

Rnd 6: 2 sc, 1 inc, [*4 sc, 1 inc* x 5], 2 sc = 36 sts.

Rnd 7: *5 sc, 1 inc* x 6 = 42 sts.

Rnd 8: 3 sc, 1 inc, [*6 sc, 1 inc* x 5], 3 sc = 48 sts.

Rnd 9 to 17: 48 sc (8 rnds).

Rnd 18: 3 sc, 1 dec, [*6 sc, 1 dec* x 5], 3 sc = 42 sts.

Rnd 19: 42 sc.

Rnd 20: *5 sc, 1 dec* x 6 = 36 sts.

Rnd 21: 2 sc, 1 dec, [*4 sc, 1 dec* x 5], 2 sc = 30 sts.

You are now at the front of the bird. You can now join the wings to the body. To place the wings in the right position, the flat edge should face towards the stomach, and the circular edge towards the back. Crochet in the last 4 double crochet stitches of the wings.

Rnd 22, front of the bird: 1 dec, 2 sc, 1 dec, 4 sc with first wing (crochet through both sts, = 4 loops on hook).

Bird's back: 1 dec, 2 sc, 1 dec, 2 sc, 1 dec, sc with first wing (crochet through both sts, = 4 loops on hook).

Front of the bird: 2 sc, 1 dec, 2 sc = 24 sts.

Do not fasten off.

⇚ The wings are further apart towards the front (9 sts) than the back (7 sts).

THE HEAD:

Rnd 23 to 26: 24 sc (4 rnds).

Rnd 27: *1 dec ,2 sc* x 6 = 18 sts.

Rnd 28: *1 sc, 1 dec* x 6 = 12 sts.

Finish stuffing the head.

Rnd 29: 6 dec = 6 sts.

Fasten off, leaving a 20 cm tail. Finish with an invisible finish and weave in ends.

→» 3. THE BEAK «←

With yarn B, leave a 15 cm tail for attaching, then ch 3.

1 sl st in 2nd ch from hook, 1 hdc.

Fasten off, leaving a 15 cm tail for attaching.

The beak should be stitched at round 27 on the head. You can place this at the front centre of the head, or to one side, as if the bird was turning its head.

Fasten off and weave in ends.

«← To position the beak, I use the wings to find the correct place.

→» 4. THE EYES «←

These are located on a stitch at round 27.

2 stitches separate them from the beak. Embroider these in black making 2 points for each one.

Fasten off and weave in ends.

→» 5. THE TAIL «←

With yarn C, crochet the tail in a spiral while working both sides of the chain.

Rnd 1: 7 ch, 1 sc in 2nd ch from hook, 4 sc, 3 sc in the same stitch, then on the other side of the chain, in the other loop: 4 sc, 1 inc = 14 sts.

Rnd 2 to 4: 14 sc (3 rnds).

Rnd 5: 3 sc, 1 dec, 5 sc, 1 dec, 2 sc, = 12 sts.

Rnd 6 to 10: 12 sc (5 rnds).

Finish off with a sl st. Fasten off, leaving a 15 cm tail. Close off with an invisible finish and weave in end. Leave to one side.

Pin the tail flat between rounds 8 and 9 to the back of the body, ensuring it is central to the head and wings. Stitch it tightly to the top and bottom.

Fasten off and weave in ends.

FREDDY
❧ THE FUNNY FOX ❧

Freddy just loves to have fun. He lives in the Sahara and when you are in the desert, everything can be a little boring without a touch of humour and imagination. Everyone laughs out loud at his jokes.

YOU WILL NEED:

1 x 2.25 mm crochet hook
Krea Deluxe organic cotton yarn:
• 14 g or 47 m Cream 02 (yarn A)
• 12 g or 40 m Golden Yellow 06 (yarn B)
• 60 cm Black 28
Polyester wadding

METHOD

⇢ All of the pieces are crocheted in a spiral using a magic ring.

⇢ Begin by crocheting the arms and the first leg to join these to the body when needed. The second leg, body and head are then crocheted to the body.

⇢ The snout and ears are crocheted last.

→» 1. THE ARMS «←

You should crochet the arms without stuffing. Make 2.

With yarn A:

Rnd 1: 6 sc into a magic ring. Pull ring closed.

Rnd 2: 6 inc = 12 sts.

Rnd 3 to 13: 12 sc (11 rnds).

Rnd 14: *1 dec, 4 sc* x 2 = 10 sts.

Rnd 15: close off the opening of the arms with 4 sc.

Fasten off, leaving a 15 cm tail. Weave in ends. Place arms to one side.

→» 2. THE LEGS «←

1ST LEG:

With yarn A:

Rnd 1: 5 sc into a magic ring. Pull ring closed.

Rnd 2: 5 inc = 10 sts.

Rnd 3: *1 sc, 1 inc* x 5 = 15 sts.

Rnd 4 to 9: 15 sc (6 rnds).

Finish off with 1 sl st. Fasten off, leaving a 15 cm tail. Close off with an invisible finish and weave in end.

2ND LEG:

With yarn A, repeat the same steps as for the 1st leg, but stop after round 9 but do not crochet the slip stitch.

Yarn over the last single crochet with yarn B, keeping 20 cm at the end of the yarn.

Fasten off yarn A.

→» 3. THE BODY «←

With yarn B: you can join the legs to the body.

Rnd 10: 9 sc (front of 2nd leg), 2 ch without tightening (= crotch), 15 sc (in the 1st leg), 2 sc (in only 1 loop of the 2 sl st), 6 sc (back of the 2nd leg) = 34 sts.

Now, the stitch marker is located on the side of the body.

Rnd 11: 9 sc, 2 sc (in the other loop of the 2 sl st), 23 sc = 34 sts.

After the next round, use the yarn B tail left from the 1st leg to hide any holes in the crotch. You can then stuff the legs. The body and head can be stuffed as you work or at the end, as you prefer.

Rnd 12 to 26: 34 sc (15 rnds).

Rnd 27: [*7 sc, 1 dec* x 3], 5 sc, 1 dec = 30 sts.

Rnd 28: 2 sc, 1 dec, [*6 sc, 1 dec* x 3], 2 sc = 26 sts.

Rnd 29: 2 sc, 1 dec, 12 sc, 1 dec, 8 sc = 24 sts.

You are now on the fox's back. On the next round, you can crochet the arms to the body.

Rnd 30: 1 sc, 4 sc with one arm for each sc (insert the hook in 1 st on the arm and 1 st on the body = 4 loops), 4 dec, 4 sc with the other arm (worked same as first arm), 3 dec. = 17 sts.

Move the stitch marker to last stitch completed (= new starting point of the rounds), now crochet a 4th dec = 16 sts.

«← Depending on how you crochet, the arms may appear a little off-centre. If so, you need to change their position, while keeping an identical number of stitches.

Rnd 31: 13 inc, 2 sc, 1 inc = 30 sts.

Finish stuffing the body. Do not fasten off.

⇒ 4. THE HEAD ⇐

Rnd 32: 2 sc, 1 inc, [*4 sc, 1 inc* x 5], 2 sc = 36 sts.

Rnd 33: *5 sc, 1 inc* x 6 = 42 sts.

Rnd 34 to 41: 42 sc (8 rnds).

Rnd 42: *5 sc, 1 dec* x 6 = 36 sts.

Rnd 43: 2 sc, 1 dec, [*4 sc, 1 dec* x 5], 2 sc = 30 sts.

Rnd 44: *3 sc, 1 dec* x 6 = 24 sts.

Rnd 45: 1 sc, 1 dec, [*2 sc, 1 dec* x 5], 1 sc = 18 sts.

Rnd 46: *1 sc, 1 dec* x 6 = 12 sts.

Finish stuffing the head.

Rnd 47: 6 dec = 6 sts.

Fasten off, leaving a 20 cm tail. Finish with an invisible finish and weave in ends.

⇒ 5. THE SNOUT ⇐

With yarn A:

Rnd 1: 6 sc into a magic ring. Pull ring closed.

Rnd 2: *1 sc, 1 inc* x 3 = 9 sts.

Rnd 3: *2 sc, 1 inc* x 3 = 12 sts.

Finish with 2 sl st. Fasten off, leaving a 35 cm tail for attaching. Close off with an invisible finish and weave in end.

Pin the snout to the head between rounds 33 and 37, ensuring it is central to the neck and giving it a triangular shape, with the tip facing upwards. Stitch it and partially stuff before closing off the stitch. Fasten off and weave in ends.

⇒ 6. THE EYES AND SNOUT ⇐

The eyes are placed on a stitch at round 37 and spaced 5 stitches apart. Embroider 3 vertical points in black for each eye.

The snout is on round 1 of the snout. Embroider 3 vertical points.

Fasten off and weave in ends.

⇒ 7. THE EARS ⇐

With yarn A:

Rnd 1: 6 sc into a magic ring. Pull ring closed.

Rnd 2: *1 sc, 1 inc* x 3 = 9 sts.

Rnd 3: 9 sc.

Rnd 4: *2 sc, 1 inc* x 3 = 12 sts.

Rnd 5: 12 sc.

Rnd 6: *3 sc, 1 inc* x 3 = 15 sts.

Rnd 7: *4 sc, 1 inc* x 3 = 18 sts.

Rnd 8: *5 sc, 1 inc* x 3 = 21 sts.

Rnd 9 to 20: 21 sc (12 rnds).

Finish off with 1 sl st. Fasten off, leaving a 30 cm tail for attaching. Close off with an invisible finish.

Flatten the ears and pin them to the head folding them forwards and rounding them off to the rear. The bottom of the ears are at round 40 and the top at round 45 (3 stitches separate the ears on this round). Stitch them tightly. Fasten off and weave in ends.

SNOWFLAKE
THE SKATING PENGUIN

Snowflake lives in the coldest place on earth amidst the ice and snow.
She is constantly skating from day to day. She doesn't need a sled to have
fun on the ice, but it has to be said that this gift is a big treat!

YOU WILL NEED:

1 x 2.25 mm crochet hook
Krea Deluxe organic cotton yarn:
• 11 g or 37 m Light Grey 48 (yarn A)
• 7 g or 24 m Natural 01 (yarn B)
• 7 g or 24 m Dark Grey 50 (yarn C)
• 4 metres Black 28 (yarn D)
Polyester wadding

METHOD

➻ All of the pieces are crocheted in a spiral from a
magic ring.
➻ Begin by making the feet and wings to join to the
body when needed. The body and head can then be
crocheted without fastening off..
➻ The beak (in a spiral and then in rows) and cap are
crocheted last.

⇢ 1. THE FEET ←

With yarn C:

Rnd 1: 6 sc into a magic ring. Pull ring closed.

Rnd 2: 6 inc = 12 sts

Finish off with 1 sl st. Fasten off, leaving a 15 cm tail. Close off with an invisible finish and weave in end.

⇢ 2. THE WINGS ←

With yarn A, you should crochet the wings without stuffing them. Make 2.

Rnd 1: in 1 magic ring, 6 sc

Rnd 2: 6 sc.

Rnd 3: *1 sc, 1 inc* x 3 = 9sts.

Rnd 4: 9 sc.

Rnd 5: *2 sc, 1 inc* x 3 = 12 sts.

Rnd 6 to 12: 12 sc (7 rnds).

Rnd 13: *1 dec, 4 sc* x 2 = 10 sts.

Rnd 14: 10 sc.

Rnd 15: close off the opening of the wing with 4 sc.

Fasten off, leaving a 15 cm tail. Weave in ends. Place the wings to one side.

⇢ 3. THE BODY AND HEAD ←

THE BODY:

With yarn A:

Rnd 1: 6 sc into a magic ring. Pull ring closed.

Rnd 2: 6 inc = 12 sts.

Rnd 3: *1 sc, 1 inc* x 6 = 18 sts.

Rnd 4: 1 sc, 1 inc, [*2 sc, 1 inc* x 5], 1 sc = 24 sts.

Rnd 5: *3 sc, 1 inc* x 6 = 30 sts.

On the next round, you will crochet the feet to the body.

Rnd 6: 2 sc, 1 inc, 4 sts. with first foot (for each sc, insert the hook in 1 st on the arm and 1 st on the body = 4 loops), 1 inc, 4 sc with the other foot (worked same as first foot), [*1 inc, 4 dc* x 3], 1 inc, 2 sc = 36 sts.

Rnd 7: *5 sc, 1 inc* x 6 = 42 sts.

Rnd 8: 3 sc, 1 inc, [*6 sc, 1 inc* x 5], 3 sc = 48 sts.

Rnd 9 to 20: 48 sc (12 rnds).

The body and the head may be stuffed as you go or at the end, as you prefer.

Rnd 21: 7 sc, 1 dec, [*10 sc, 1 dec* x 3], 3 sc = 44 sts.

Rnd 22: 44 sc.

Rnd 23: 7 sc, 1 dec, [*9 sc, 1 dec* x 3], 2 sc = 40 sts.

Rnd 24: 40 sc.

Rnd 25: 7 sc, 1 dec, [*8 sc, 1 dec* x 3], 1 sc = 36 sts.

Rnd 26: 2 sc, 1 dec, [*4 sc, 1 dec* x 5], 2 sc = 30 sts.

Rnd 27: *3 sc, 1 dec* x 6 = 24 sts.

You are now at the back of the penguin. On the next round, you can crochet the wings to the body.

Rnd 28: 1 sc, 4 sc with first wing (for each sc, insert the crochet in 1 st on the wing and 1 st on the body = 4 loops on hook), 8 sc, 4 sc with the other wing (worked as first wing), 7 sc (yo the last stitch with yarn B) = 24 sts.

   ← Depending on how you crochet, the wings may appear a little off-centre. If so, you need to change their position, while keeping an identical number of stitches.

Fasten off yarn A and tie the ends of yarns A and B together.

4. THE BEAK AND FRONT

With yarn D, you can begin to crochet in a spiral.

Rnd 1: in 1 magic ring, 6sc.

Rnd 2: *1 sc, 1 inc* x 3 = 9 sts.

Rnd 3: 9 sc.

Finish off with 1 sl st and 1 ch. Turn.

Continue the front crocheting in rows.

Row 1: 1 inc, 1 sc, 1 inc = 5 sts. 1 ch. Turn.

Row 2: 1 inc, 3 sc, 1 inc = 7 st. 1 ch. Turn.

Row 3: 1 inc, 5 sc, 1 inc = 9 sts. 1 ch, then turn.

Row 4: 1 inc, 7 sc, 1 inc = 11 sts.

Fasten off leaving a 35 cm tail for attaching.

Pin the middle of the 1st round of the beak (magic ring) and insert it into the centre of the head between rounds 34 and 35. The front (section crocheted in rows) should be pinned towards the top at round 39.

The beak may be partially stuffed. Stitch around the edge.

5. THE EYES

These should be placed at 2 or 3 stitches from the beak, on a stitch at round 35. For each eye, embroider 2 vertical points + 1 horizontal point above in black.

Fasten off and weave in ends.

THE HEAD:

With yarn B:

Rnd 29: *3 sc, 1 inc* x 6 = 30 sts.

Rnd 30: 2 sc, 1 inc, [*4 sc, 1 inc* x 5], 2 sc = 36 sts.

Rnd 31: *5 sc, 1 inc* x 6 = 42 sts.

Rnd 32 to 39: 42 sc (8 rnds).

Rnd 40: *5 sc, 1 dec* = 36 sts.

Rnd 41: 2 sc, 1 dec, [*4 sc, 1 dec* x 5], 2 sc = 30 sts.

Rnd 42: *3 sc, 1 dec* x 6 = 24 sts.

Rnd 43: 1 sc, 1 dec, [*2 sc, 1 dec* x 5], 1 sc = 18 sts.

Rnd 44: *1 dec, 1 sc* x 6 = 12 sts.

Finish stuffing the head.

Rnd 45: 6 dec = 6 sts.

Fasten off, leaving a 20 cm tail. Finish with an invisible finish and weave in ends.

⟶ 6. THE CAP ⟵

With yarn C:

Rnd 1: 6 dc in magic ring.

Rnd 2: 6 inc = 12 sts.

Rnd 3: *1 sc, 1 inc* x 6 = 18 sts.

Rnd 4: 1 sc, 1 inc, [*2 sc, 1 inc* x 5], 1 sc = 24 sts.

Rnd 5: *3 sc, 1 inc* x 6 = 30 sts.

Rnd 6: 2 sc, 1 inc, [*4 sc, 1 inc* x 5], 2 sc = 36 sts.

Rnd 7: *5 sc, 1 inc* x 6 = 42 sts.

Rnd 8 to 16: 42 sc (9 rnds).

⟵ Depending on how you crochet and the yarn chosen, you may need to crochet more or less rounds. You should, therefore, try the cap on the penguin, and keep adding rounds until you are happy.

Finish off with 1 sl st. Fasten off, leaving a 40 cm tail for attaching. Close off with an invisible finish.

Fix the cap on the head with pins and stitch it with several stitches around the head.

OSCAR
❧ THE BUSY BEAVER ❧

Oscar is a busy beaver, just like his parents. Everything he touches turns to gold. Later in life, he wants to become an architect and specialize in wooden constructions. He will build a magnificent lakeside house.

YOU WILL NEED:

1 x 2.25 mm crochet hook
Krea Deluxe organic cotton yarn:
• 14 g or 47 m Earth Brown 29 (yarn A)
• 3 g or 10 m Black 28 (yarn B)
• 40 cm Natural 01
Polyester wadding

METHOD

⇢ All pieces are crocheted in a spiral using a magic ring.

⇢ Begin with the tail, arms and first leg to join to the body when needed. The second leg, body and head can then be crocheted without fastening off.

⇢ The ears should be crocheted last.

⇢ 1. THE TAIL ⇠

With yarn B, you should crochet the tail without stuffing.

Rnd 1: 6 sc into a magic ring. Pull ring closed.

Rnd 2: 6 inc = 12 sts.

Rnd 3: *3 sc, 1 inc* x 3 = 15 sts.

Rnd 4 to 10: 15 sc (7 rnds).

Rnd 11: *3 sc, 1 dec* x 3 = 12 sts.

Rnd 12 and 13: 12 sc (2 rnds).

Rnd 14: *4 sc, 1 dec* x 2 = 10 sts.

Rnd 15: 10 sc.

Rnd 16: *3 sc, 1 dec* x 2 = 8 sts.

Rnd 17: [*1 sc, 1 dec* x 2], 1 dec = 5 sts.

Rnd 18: close off the opening of the tail with 2 sc. 1 ch, turn.

Rnd 19: 2 sc.

Fasten off, leaving a 15 cm tail. Weave in ends. Flatten the tail and set aside.

⇢ 2. THE ARMS ⇠

With yarn A, you should crochet the arms without stuffing. Make 2.

Rnd 1: 6 sc into a magic ring. Pull ring closed.

Rnd 2: 6 inc = 12 sts.

Rnd 3 to 10: 12 sc (8 rnds).

Rnd 11: *1 dec, 4 sc* x 2 = 10 sts.

Rnd 12: close off the opening of the arms with 4 sc.

Fasten off, leaving a 15 cm tail. Weave in ends. Place the arms to one side.

⇢ 3. THE LEGS ⇠

1ˢᵀ LEG:

With yarn B:

Rnd 1: 6 sc into a magic ring. Pull ring closed.

Rnd 2: 6 inc = 12 sts.

Rnd 3: *3 sc, 1 inc* x 3 = 15 sts.

Rnd 4 (BLO): 15 sc.

Finish off with 1 sl st. Fasten off, leaving a 15 cm tail for securing crotch.

2ᴺᴰ LEG:

With yarn B:

Repeat the same steps as for the 1ˢᵗ leg, but stop after round 4 and do not crochet the slip stitch. Yarn over for the last single crochet with yarn A. Fasten off yarn B.

Continue with yarn A.

⇢ 4. THE BODY AND HEAD ⇠

You can now begin the body by joining the legs. Place a stitch marker in the 1ˢᵗ stitch.

Rnd 5: 8 sc (front of 2ⁿᵈ leg), 4 ch without tightening (= crotch), 15 sc (in the 1ˢᵗ leg), 4 sc (in only 1 loop of 2 sl st), 7 sc (back of the 2ⁿᵈ leg) = 38 sts.

Now the stitch marker is on the side of the body.

Rnd 6: 8 sc, 4 sc (in the other loop of the 4 ch), 26 sc = 38 sts.

On the next round, you will crochet the tail to the body.

Rnd 7: 1 inc, 18 sc, 1 inc, 8 sc, 2 sc with the tail (for each sc, insert the crochet in 1 st of the tail and 1 st of the body = 4 loops on hook), 8 sc = 40 sts.

Rnd 8 to 19: 40 sc (12 rnds).

Stuff the body and head as you go or at the end, as you prefer.

Rnd 20: 3 sc, 1 dec, 17 sc, 1 dec, 16 sc = 38 sts.

Rnd 21: 38 sc.

Rnd 22: 3 sc, 1 dec, 16 sc, 1 dec, 15 sc = 36 sts.

Rnd 23: 36 sc.

Rnd 24: 3 sc, 1 dec, 15 sc, 1 dec, 14 sc = 34 sts.

Rnd 25: 34 sc.

You are now on the beaver's back. On the next round, you can crochet the arms to the body.

Rnd 26: 2 sc, 4 sc with first arm (for each sc, insert the crochet in 1 st on the arm and 1 st on the body = 4 loops on hook), 13 sc, 4 sc with the other arm (work as first arm), 11 sc = 34 sts.

≪ Depending on how you crochet, the arms may appear a little off-centre. If so, you need to change their position, while keeping an identical number of stitches.

Rnd 27: 3 sc, 1 dec, 15 sc, 1 dec, 12 sc = 32 sts.

Rnd 28: 32 sc.

Rnd 29: 3 sc, 1 dec, 14 sc, 1 dec, 11 sc = 30 sts.

Rnd 30: 30 sc.

Rnd 31: 3 sc, 1 dec, 13 sc, 1 dec, 10 sc = 28 sts.

Rnd 32 and 33: 28 sc (2 rnds).

Rnd 34: *5 sc, 1 dec* x 4 = 24 sts.

Rnd 35: *2 sc, 1 dec* x 6 = 18 sts.

Rnd 36: *1 sc, 1 dec* x 6 = 12 sts.

Finish stuffing the head.

Rnd 37: 6 dec = 6 sts.

Fasten off, leaving a 20 cm tail. Finish with an invisible finish and weave in ends.

⇢ 5. THE EYES, SNOUT AND MOUTH ⇠

With yarn B (4 loops):

The eyes should be located on a stitch at round 33 and are separated by 5 stitches. They should each be made up of 2 vertical points.

The snout is located in the centre of round 32. Embroider 4 or 5 vertical points.

Fasten off and weave in ends.

With the Natural yarn (2 strands), embroider the teeth at round 30 making 2 small vertical points. Fasten off and weave in ends.

With yarn B (2 strands), embroider the mouth forming a Y-shape on the back just above the teeth. Fasten off and weave in ends.

⇢ 6. THE EARS ⇠

Keep at least 10 cm of yarn at the end of the magic ring, this can be used to fasten off the yarn.

Rnd 1: 5 sc into a magic ring. Pull ring closed.

Fasten off, leaving a 15 cm tail for attaching.

Pin the ears to the sides of the head (round 34) and stitch tightly. Fasten off and weave in ends.

DONNIE
❧ THE ROMANTIC DONKEY ☙

Donnie loves running across vast prairies to take in the wonder of the nature all around, the smell of the grass, the songs of the birds. Sometimes, he just stands still, with his eyes closed. Not sleeping! Just reciting poetry.

YOU WILL NEED:

1 x 2.25 mm crochet hook
Krea Deluxe organic cotton yarn
20 g or 66 m Warm Light Grey 17 (yarn A)
• 2 g or 7 m Dark Grey 50 (yarn B)
• 3 m Natural 01 (yarn C)
• 60 cm Black 28
Polyester wadding

METHOD

↠ All pieces are worked in a spiral using a magic ring.

↠ Begin with the arms and the first leg to be joined to the body when needed. The second leg, body and head can then be crocheted without cutting the yarn.

↠ The snout and ears are crocheted last.

⇥ 1. THE ARMS ⇤

With yarn B:

You should crochet the arms without stuffing them. Make 2.

Rnd 1: 6 sc into a magic ring. Pull ring closed.

Rnd 2: 6 inc = 12 sts.

Rnd 3 (BLO): 12 sc.

Rnd 4: 12 sc (yarn over the last stich with yarn A).

Cut yarn B and tie to the end of yarn A.

With yarn A:

Rnd 5 to 15: 12 sc (11 rnds).

Rnd 16: *1 dec, 4 sc* x 2 = 10 sts.

Rnd 17: close off the opening of the arms with 4 sc.

Fasten off, leaving a 15 cm tail. Weave in ends. Place the arms to one side.

⇥ 2. THE LEGS ⇤

1ST LEG:

With yarn B:

Rnd 1: 5 sc into a magic ring. Pull ring closed.

Rnd 2: 5 inc = 10 sts.

Rnd 3: *1 sc, 1 inc* x 5 = 15 sts.

Rnd 4 (BLO): 15 sc.

Rnd 5: 15 sc (yarn over the last stitch with yarn A).

Fasten off yarn B and tie to the end of yarn A.

With yarn A:

Rnd 6 to 11: 15 sc (6 rnds).

Add 2 sc to the end of round 11 to offset the change of colour towards the crotch.

Finish with 1 sl st. Finish off with a sl st. Fasten off, leaving a 20 cm tail and leave to one side.

2ND LEG:

Repeat the same steps as for the 1st leg, but stop after round 11 and do not crochet the 2 additional sc or sl st and do not fasten off.

⇥ 3. THE BODY ⇤

You can now begin the body by joining the legs. Place a stitch marker in the 1st stitch.

Rnd 12: 10 sc (front of 2nd leg), 2 ch without tightening (= crotch), 15 sc (in the 1st leg), 2 sc (in only 1 loop of the 2 ch), 5 sc (back of the 2nd leg) = 34 sts.

Now, the stitch marker is on the side of the body.

Rnd 13: 10 sc, 2 sc (in the other loop of the 2 ch), 22 sc = 34 sts.

After the next round, use the yarn A tail left from the 1st leg to hide any holes in the crotch. You can then stuff the legs. The body and head can be stuffed as you work or at the end, as you prefer.

Rnd 14 to 28: 34 sc (15 rnds).

Rnd 29: [*7 sc, 1 dec* x 3], 5 sc, 1dec = 30 sts.

Rnd 30: 2 sc, 1 dec, [*6 sc, 1 dec* x 3], 2 sc = 26 sts.

Rnd 31: 2 sc, 1 dec, 12 sc, 1 dec, 8 sc = 24 sts.

You are now on the donkey's back. On the next round, you can crochet the arms to the body,

Rnd 32: 2 sc, 4 sc with first arm (for each sc, insert the crochet hook in 1 st on the arm and 1 st on the body = 4 loops on hook), 4 dec, 4 sc with the other arm (work as first arm), 3 dec = 17 sts.

← Depending on how you crochet, the arms may appear a little off-centre. If so, you need to change their position, while keeping an identical number of stitches.

Rnd 33: 1 dec, 13 inc, 2 sc = 29 sts.

Finish stuffing the body. Do not fasten off.

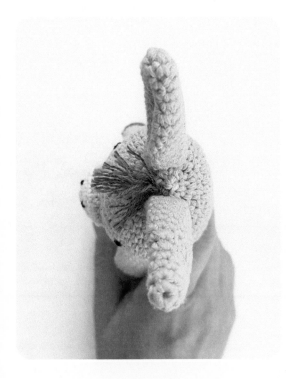

→» 4. THE HEAD «←

Rnd 34: 2 inc, [*4 sc, 1 inc* x 5], 2 sc = 36 sts.

Rnd 35: *5 sc, 1 inc* x 6 = 42 sts.

Rnd 36 to 43: 42 sc (8 rnds).

Rnd 44: *5 sc, 1 dec* x 6 = 36 sts.

Rnd 45: 2 sc, 1 dec [*4 sc, 1 dec* x 5], 2 sc = 30 sts.

Rnd 46: *3 sc, 1 dec* x 6 = 24 sts.

Rnd 47: 1 sc, 1 dec, [*2 sc, 1 dec* x 5], 1 sc = 18 sts.

Rnd 48: *1 sc, 1 dec* x 4 = 12 sts.

Finish stuffing the head.

Rnd 49: 6 dec = 6 sts.

Fasten off, leaving a 20 cm tail. Finish with an invisible finish and weave in ends.

→» 5. THE SNOUT «←

With yarn C:

Rnd 1: in 1 magic ring, 6sc.

Rnd 2: 6 inc = 12 sts.

Rnd 3: *1 sc, 1 inc* x 6 = 18 sts.

Rnd 4: 18 sc (yarn over the last stitch with yarn A).

With yarn A:

Rnd 5: *2 sc, 1 inc* x 6 = 24 sts.

Fasten off yarn C and tie to the end of yarn A.

Finish off with 1 sl st. Fasten off, leaving a 35 cm tail for attaching. Close off with an invisible finish.

Pin the snout to the head between rounds 34 and 41, ensuring it is central in relation to the neck. Stitch it by stuffing partially before then closing off your stitch.

Fasten off and weave in ends.

→» 6. THE EARS «←

With yarn A:

Rnd 1: 6 sc into a magic ring. Pull ring closed.

Rnd 2: *1 sc, 1 inc* x 3 = 9 sts.

Rnd 3 and 4: 9 sc (2 rnds).

Rnd 5: *2 sc, 1 inc* x 3 = 12 sts.

Rnd 6: *2 sc, 1 inc* x 4 = 16 sts.

Rnd 7 to 14: 16 sc (8 rnds).

Finish off with 1 sl st. Fasten off, leaving a 30 cm tail for attaching. Close off with an invisible finish.

Flatten the ears and fold the arms in two to join at the edges with a few stitches.

Pin them to the top of the head leaving a small gap (rounds 49 and 50) between the two.

Stitch them firmly.

Fasten off and weave in ends.

➳➳ 7. THE EYES, NOSTRILS AND HAIR ⇇⇇

The eyes are located on a stitch at round 41 and are spaced 10 stitches apart. Embroider these in black with 3 vertical points.

The nostrils are located on round 2 of the snout: embroider 2 vertical points for each, spaced 2 stitches apart. Fasten off and weave in ends.

For the hair, use the dark grey yarn and cut 4 or 5 lengths of 8 cm yarn. Fold them in two to form a loop.

To fasten off each length of yarn, insert the crochet hook through 2 contiguous holes at the top of the head, then pull the loop through by 1 to 2 cm. Pass the 2 ends of the yarn through the loop and pull. Cut some of the loops to measure around 1.5 to 2 cm. To fasten off, make some stitches on the knots with a thread of the same colour.

⇇⇇ To separate the loops of the hair, simply comb them!

RICKY, NICKY AND MICKY

THE NAUGHTY KITTENS

Ricky, Nicky and Micky love to play hide and seek. They never stop messing around! They climb up the curtains, knock over the ornaments and mess up the beds ... The house is a fun playground which they quickly turn upside down!

YOU WILL NEED:

1 x 2.25 mm crochet hook
Polyester wadding
Ricorumi cotton yarn: 60 cm Green 048 (eyes)
Krea Deluxe organic cotton yarn:
• 60 cm Black 28 (pupils and snout)

Ricky:

• 21 g or 70 m Linen 46 (yarn A, body and head)

• 7 g or 23 m Mustard Yellow 09 (yarn B, stripes and ends of the arms and legs)

Nicky:

• 21 g or 70 m Mustard Yellow 09 (yarn A, body and head)

• 7 g or 20 m Dark Brown 29 (yarn B, stripes)

• 3 m Croissant 53 (yarn C, ends of arms and legs)

Micky:

• 22 g or 73 m Croissant 53 (yarn A, body and head)

• 7 g or 20 m Dark Brown 29 (yarn B, stripes)

RICKY

NICKY

MICKY

METHOD

→» All of the pieces are worked in a spiral using a magic ring.

→» Begin by crocheting the arms and the first leg so they are ready to be joined to the body. The second leg, the body and head are then crocheted without fastening off.

→» The ears are crocheted last.

→» 1. THE ARMS «←

You can crochet the arms without stuffing them. Make 2.

Begin with yarn B for Ricky (yarn C for Nicky, yarn A for Micky).

Rnd 1: 6 sc into a magic ring. Pull ring closed.

Rnd 2: 6 inc = 12 m.

Rnd 3: 12 sc (if you have used yarn B or C, yarn over the last stitch with yarn A).

If you have chosen yarn C, fasten it off.

Now alternate between 3 rounds with yarn A, 1 round with yarn B, changing colour when yarning over on the last stitch of the previous round.

Rnd 4 to 14: 12 sc (11 rnds: 3 with yarn A, 1 with yarn B, 3 with yarn A, 1 with yarn B, 3 with yarn A).

Rnd 15, yarn B: *1 dec, 4 sc* x 2 = 10 sts (yarn over the last stitch with yarn A).

Rnd 16, yarn A: 1 sc (this stitch then allows you to offset the change of colour to one side, if you need to), then close off the opening with 4 sc.

Fasten off both yarns, leaving a 15 cm tail. Weave in ends. Place the arms to one side.

→» 2. THE LEGS «←

1ST LEG:

Begin with yarn B for Ricky (yarn C for Nicky, yarn A for Micky).

Rnd 1: 5 sc into a magic ring. Pull ring closed.

Rnd 2: 5 inc = 10 sts.

Rnd 3: *1 sc, 1 inc* x 5 = 15 sts (if you have used yarn B or C, yarn over the last stitch with yarn A).

If you have chosen yarn C, cut it and tie off.

Now, alternate 3 rounds with yarn A, 1 round with yarn B, changing colour when yarning over the last stitch of the previous round.

Rnd 4 to 9: 15 sc (6 rnds: 3 with yarn A, 1 with yarn B, 2 with yarn A).

Finish off with 1 sl st. Fasten off yarn B. Fasten off yarn A, leaving a 20 cm tail. Place to one side.

2ND LEG:

Repeat the same steps as for the 1st leg, but stop after round 9: do not do the sl st or fasten off.

⇒⇒ 3. THE BODY ⇐⇐

You can now begin the body by joining the legs. Place a stitch marker in the 1st stitch.

Rnd 10, yarn A: 9 sc (front of the 2nd leg), 2 ch without tightening (= crotch), 15 sc (in the 1st leg), 2 sc (in only 1 loop of the 2 ch), 6 sc (back of the 2nd leg) = 34 sts (yarn over the last stitch with yarn B).

Now the stitch marker is located on the side of the body.

Rnd 11, yarn B: 9 sc, 2 sc (in the other loop of the 2 ch), 23 sc = 34 sts (yarn over the last stitch with yarn A).

After the next round, use the yarn A tail left from the 1st leg to hide any holes in the crotch. You can then stuff the legs. The body and head can be stuffed as you work or at the end, as you prefer.

Continue to alternate 3 rounds with yarn A, 1 round with yarn B, changing colour when yarning over for the final stitch on the previous round.

Rnd 12 to 26: 34 sc (15 rnds: 3 with yarn A, 1 with yarn B, 3 with yarn A).

Rnd 27, yarn B: [*7 sc, 1 dec* x 3], 5 sc, 1 dec = 30 sts (yarn over the last stitch with yarn A).

Rnd 28, yarn A: 2 sc, 1 dec, [*6 sc, 1 dec* x 3], 2 sc = 26 sts.

Cut yarn B and tie off, then continue only with yarn A.

Rnd 29: 2 sc, 1 dec, 12 sc, 1 dec, 8 sc = 24 sts.

You are now on the kitten's back. On the next round, you can crochet the arms to the body.

Place the arms in the correct direction (change of colour towards the back).

Rnd 30: 1 sc, 4 sc with first arm (for each dc, insert the hook in 1 st of the arm and 1 st of the body = 4 loops on hook), 4 dec, 4 sc with the other arm (work as first arm), 3 dec (1 st will be left on the round) = 17 sts. Move the stitch marker 1 st to the left (= new starting point for the rounds) and crochet a 4th dec = 16 sts.

⇐⇐ Depending on how you crochet, the arms may appear a little off-centre. If so, you need to change their position, while keeping an identical number of stitches.

Rnd 31: 13 inc, 2 sc, 1 inc = 30 sts.

Finish stuffing the body. Do not fasten off.

⇒⇒ 4. THE HEAD ⇐⇐

Rnd 32: 2 sc, 1 inc [*4 sc, 1 inc* x 5] 2 sc = 36 sts.

Rnd 33: *5 sc, 1 inc* x 6 = 42 sts.

Rnd 34 to 41: 42 sc (8 rnds).

Rnd 42: *5 sc, 1 dec* x 6 = 36 sts.

Rnd 43: 2 sc, 1 dec, [*4 sc, 1 dec* x 5], 2 sc = 30 sts.

Rnd 44: *3 sc, 1 dec* x 6 = 24 sts.

Rnd 45: 1 sc, 1 dec, [*2 sc, 1 dec* x 5], 1 dc = 18 sts.

Rnd 46: *1 sc, 1 dec* x 4 = 12 sts.

Finish stuffing the head.

Rnd 47: 6 dec = 6 sts.

Fasten off, leaving a 20 cm tail. Finish with an invisible finish and weave in ends.

⇥ 5. THE EARS ⇤

With yarn A:

Rnd 1: 6 sc into a magic ring. Pull ring closed.

Rnd 2: *1 sc, 1 inc* x 3 = 9 sts.

Rnd 3: *2 sc, 1 inc* x 3 = 12 sts.

Rnd 4: *3 sc, 1 inc* x 3 = 15 sts.

Finish off with 1 sl st. Fasten off, leaving a 30 cm tail for attaching. Close off with an invisible finish.

Flatten the ears and pin them to the head, folding a little towards the front to accentuate the tip. The bottom of the ears should be at round 42 and the top at round 46 (3 or 4 stitches separate the ears at this round). Stitch them tightly.

Fasten off and weave in ends.

⇥ 6. THE FACE ⇤

The stripes are formed of 3 rows of pointed stitches to the front. Embroider with yarn B (4 loops).

The eyes are located at round 37 and spaced out by 7 stitches: embroider using green yarn (2 loops) 4 small vertical points + 1 diagonal point for each eye.

Using the black yarn (1 loop):

The snout is between round 35 and 36: make 4 small horizontal points. Then pass the needle beneath round 35 to form the mouth. Make 1 wide horizontal point 3 stitches wide + 1 small vertical point covering the mouth and tip of the snout.

The pupils are each made up of 2 small vertical points in the middle of each eye.

Fasten off by colour and weave in ends.

ZEBBY

 ## THE PRETTY ZEBRA

Zebby certainly stands out in the Savana. Her pretty stripes don't just look nice, they apparently help protect her from the sun's rays as well as the nasty insects. Beauty and intelligence combined to perfection.

YOU WILL NEED:

1 x 2.25 mm crochet hook
Krea Deluxe organic cotton yarn:
• 15 g or 50 m of Natural 01 (yarn A)
• 7 g or 24 m Black 28 (yarn B)
• A few metres of Coal Grey 51 (yarn C)
Polyester wadding

METHOD

⇢ All pieces are crocheted in a spiral using a magic ring.

⇢ Start by crocheting the arms and the first leg to join them to the body when needed. The second leg, the body and the head are then crocheted without fastening off.

⇢ The snout and ears are then crocheted last.

⇝ 1. THE ARMS ⇜

Using yarn B, you can begin to crochet the arms without stuffing them. Make 2.

Rnd 1: 6 sc into a magic ring. Pull ring closed.

Rnd 2: 6 inc = 12 sts.

Rnd 3 (BLO): 12 sc.

Rnd 4: 12 sc (yarn over the last stitch with yarn A).

Now you can alternate the colours (don't forget to change colour when yarning over the last stitch of the previous row).

Rnd 5 to 15: 12 sc (11 rnds: 3 with yarn A, 1 with yarn B, 3 with yarn A, 1 with yarn B, 3 with yarn A).

Rnd 16, yarn B: *1 dec, 4 sc* x 2 = 10 sts (yarn over the last stitch with yarn A).

Rnd 17, yarn A: 1 sc (this stitch allows you to offset the colour change), then close off with 4 sc.

Fasten off, leaving a 15 cm tail with yarn A. Weave in ends.

⇝ 2. THE LEGS ⇜

1ʳᵉ LEG:

Begin with yarn B.

Rnd 1: 5 sc into a magic ring. Pull ring closed.

Rnd 2: 5 inc = 10 sts.

Rnd 3: *1 sc, 1 inc* x 5 = 15 sts.

Rnd 4 (BLO): 15 sc.

Rnd 5: 15 sc (yarn over the last stitch with yarn A).

Now you can alternate the colours. Be sure to change the colour when yarning over the last stitch of the previous round.

Rnd 6 to 11: 15 sc (6 rnds: 3 with yarn A, 1 with yarn B, 2 with yarn A). Add 2 sc at the end of round 11 to offset the colour change towards the crotch.

Finish off with 1 sc. Fasten off yarn B, leaving a 15 cm tail. Faten off yarn A, leaving a 20 cm tail for stitching the crotch. Leave to one side.

2ᴺᴰ LEG:

Repeat the same steps as for the 1ˢᵗ leg, but stop after round 11: do not do additional 2 sc or sl st. Do not fasten off.

⇝ 3. THE BODY ⇜

With yarn A: you can now begin the body by joining the legs. Place a stitch marker in the 1ˢᵗ stitch.

Rnd 12: 9 sc (front of the 2ⁿᵈ leg), 2 ch without tightening (= crotch), 15 sc (in the 1ˢᵗ leg), 2 sc (in only 1 of the 2 ch), 6 sc (back of the 2ⁿᵈ leg) = 34 sts (yarn over the last stitch with yarn B).

Now the stitch marker is on the side of the body.

With yarn B:

Rnd 13: 9 sc, 2 sc (in the other loop of the 2 ch), 23 sc = 34 sts (yarn over the last stitch with yarn A).

After the next round, use the yarn A tail left from the 1ˢᵗ leg to hide any holes in the crotch. You can then stuff the legs. The body and head can be stuffed as you work or at the end, as you prefer.

⇜ For each colour change, do not forget to yarn over the last stitch on the previous round.

≪← Depending on how you crochet, the arms may appear a little off-centre. If so, you need to change their position, while keeping an identical number of stitches.

Rnd 34: 1 dec, 13 inc, 2 sc = 29 sts.

Finish stuffing the body. Do not fasten off.

Rnd 14 to 28: 34 sc (15 rnds: *3 with yarn A, 1 with yarn B* x 3 + 3 with yarn A) (yarn over the last stitch with yarn B).

Rnd 29, yarn B: [*7 sc, 1 dec* x 3], 5 sc, 1 dec = 30 sts (yarn over the last stitch with yarn A).

Rnd 30, yarn A: 2 sc, 1 dec, [*6 sc, 1 dec* x 3], 2 sc. = 26 sts.

Fasten off yarn B, then continue only with yarn A.

Rnd 31: 2 sc, 1 dec, 12 sc, 1 dec, 8 sc = 24 sts.

Rnd 32: 24 sc.

You are now on the zebra's back. On the next round, you can crochet the arms to the body.

Rnd 33: 2 sc, 4 sc with first arm (for each sc, insert the crochet hook into 1 st on the arm and 1 st on the body = 4 loops on hook), 4 dec, 4 sc with the other arm (work as first arm), 3 dec = 17 sts

→» 4. THE HEAD ≪←

Rnd 35: [*8 sc, 1 inc* x 3], 2 sc = 32 sts.

Rnd 36: 32 sc.

Rnd 37: 5 sc, 1 inc, [*9 sc, 1 inc* x 2], 6 sc = 35 sts.

Rnd 38: 35 sc.

Rnd 39: *4 sc, 1 inc* x 7 = 42 sts.

Rnd 40 to 44: 42 sc (5 rnds).

Rnd 45: *5 sc, 1 dec* x 6 = 36 sts.

Rnd 46: 2 sc, 1 dec, [*4 sc, 1 dec* x 5], 2 sc = 30 sts.

Rnd 47: *3 sc, 1 dec* x 6 = 24 sts.

Rnd 48: 1 sc, 1 dec, [*2 sc, 1 dec* x 5] 1 sc = 18 sts.

Rnd 49: *1 sc, 1 dec* x 6 = 12 sts.

Finish stuffing the head.

Rnd 50: 6 dec = 6 sts.

Fasten off, leaving a 20 cm tail. Finish with an invisible finish and weave in ends.

⇾⇾ 5. THE SNOUT ⇽⇽

Begin with yarn C.

Rnd 1: 6 sc into a magic ring. Pull ring closed.

Rnd 2: 6 inc = 12 sts.

Rnd 3: *1 sc, 1 inc* x 6 = 18 sts (yarn over the last stitch with yarn A).

Rnd 4: with yarn A: 18 sc.

Fasten off yarn C.

Rnd 5: *2 sc, 1 inc* x 6 = 24 sts.

Finish with 1 sl st. Fasten off yarn A, leaving a 35 cm tail. Finish with an invisible finish.

Pin the snout to the head between rounds 34 and 41, ensuring it is central to the neck.

Stitch and partially stuff before closing off your stitches.

Fasten off and weave in ends.

⇾⇾ 6. THE EARS ⇽⇽

You can crochet the ears without stuffing them.

Rnd 1, yarn B: 6 sc in magic ring, (yarn over the last stitch with yarn A).

Rnd 2, yarn A: *1 sc, 1 inc* x 3 = 9 sts.

Fasten off yarn B and tie to the end of yarn A.

Rnd 3: 9 sc.

Rnd 4: *2 sc, 1 inc* x 3 = 12 sts.

Rnd 5 to 8: 12 sc (4 rnds).

Finish with 1 sc. Fasten off, leaving a 30 cm tail for attaching. Finish off with an invisible finish.

Flatten the ears and fold the base in two to join the edges with a few stitches. Pin each ear at rounds 47 and 48 (2 stitches separate the ears at this round). Stitch them tightly.

Fasten off and weave in ends.

⇾⇾ 7. THE EYES AND HAIR ⇽⇽

The eyes are on a stitch at round 41 and spaced 10 stitches apart. For each eye, embroider 3 vertical points + 1 horizontal point in black beneath the vertical points.

Fasten off and weave in ends.

The hair forms a straight line between the 2 ears. Cut 3 lengths of black yarn 8 cm long. Fold them in two to form a loop.

To fix each length of yarn, insert the crochet hook through 2 contiguous holes at the top of the head, then take the loop and pull out 1 to 2 cm. Pass the 2 ends of the yarn in the loop and pull.

Cut the strands of hair a little to measure around 1 cm. To fasten off, make a few stitches on the knots with a piece of thread the same colour.

HECTOR
THE HAPPY HOUND

Hector often sits in front of his house to watch the world go by,
but what he loves above all is to go on a walk. Although he walks
every day with the family, he sometimes loves to get away on his own, probably off
chasing a new smell... But he always returns home, where his heart is!

YOU WILL NEED:

1 x 2.25 mm crochet hook
Krea Deluxe organic cotton yarn:
• 23 g or 76 m Natural White 01 (yarn A)
• 5 m Croissant 53 (yarn B)
• 60 cm Black 28
Polyester wadding

METHOD

→→ This pattern has a few complex colour changes explained in detail (marks to the body and head).

→→ All pieces are crocheted in a spiral using a magic ring.

→→ Start by crocheting the arms and first leg to be joined to the body when needed. The second leg, body and head can then be crocheted without fastening off.

→→ The muzzle and ears are crocheted last.

⇥ 1. THE ARMS ⇤

You can crochet the arms without stuffing them. Make 2.

Using yarn A:

Rnd 1: 6 sc into a magic ring. Pull ring closed.

Rnd 2: 6 inc = 12 sts.

Rnd 3 to 14: 12 sc (12 rnds).

Rnd 15: *1 dec, 4 sc* x 2 = 10 sts.

Rnd 16: close off the opening of the arm with 4 sc.

Fasten off, leaving a 15 cm end. Place the arms to one side.

⇥ 2. THE LEGS ⇤

1ST LEG:

With yarn A:

Rnd 1: 5 sc into a magic ring. Pull ring closed. .

Rnd 2: 5 inc = 10 sts.

Rnd 3: *1 sc, 1 inc* x 5 = 15 sts.

Rnd 4 to 9: 15 sc (6 rnds).

Finish with 1 sl st. Fasten off leaving a 20 cm tail. Place to one side.

2ND LEG:

With yarn A:

Repeat the same steps as for the 1st leg, but stop after round 9. Do not crochet the slip stitch, do not fasten off.

⇥ 3. THE BODY ⇤

You can now begin the body by joining the legs. Place a stitch marker in the 1st stitch.

Rnd 10: 8 sc (front of the 2nd leg), 2 ch without tightening (= crotch), 15 sc (in the 1st leg), 2 sc (in only 1 loop of the ch), 7 sc (back of the 2nd leg) = 34 sts.

Now, the stitch marker is on the side of the body.

Rnd 11: 8 sc, 2 sc (in the other loop of the 2 ch), 24 sc = 34 sts.

Rnd 12: 2 sc, 1 inc, 12 sc, 1 inc, 3 sc, 1 inc, 12 sc, 1 inc, 1 sc = 38 sts.

After row 14 or 15, use the yarn tail left from the 1st leg in order to hide any holes in the crotch. You can then stuff the legs.

Rnd 13 to 15: 38 sc (3 rnds).

⇤ Watch out, as there are colour changes for 6 rounds! At each change, the yarns are hidden at the back (= inside the piece). Do not cut them or draw them through to avoid misshaping the animal.

Rnd 16: 13 sc with yarn A, 2 dc with the first yarn over using yarn A and the 2nd yarn over using yarn B (for these 2 sts) (photo 1), 5 sc with yarn B (photos 2, 3 and 4), 1 sc with the 1st yarn over with yarn B (photo 5) and the 2nd yarn over with yarn A (photo 6), 17 sc with yarn A = 38 sts.

⇤ When you crochet the 5 sc with yarn B, you need to trap the yarn at the back with a handful of stitches. This is to be used again at the end of the 5 sc, as well as the end of yarn B to tie off.

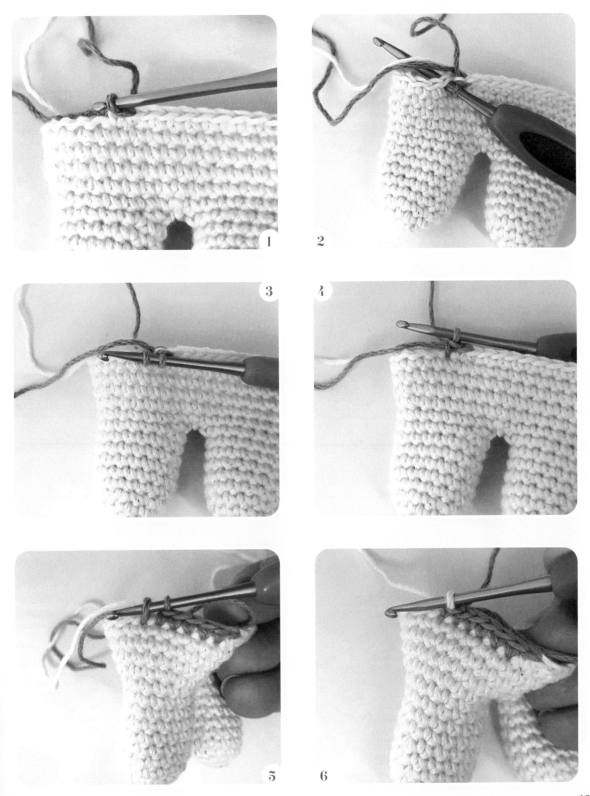

Rnd 17: 12 sc with yarn A, 2 sc with the 1ˢᵗ yarn over with yarn A and the 2ⁿᵈ yarn over with yarn B (for these 2 sts) (photos 7 and 8), 7 sc with yarn B, 1 sc with the 1ˢᵗ yarn over with yarn B (photo 9) and the 2ⁿᵈ yarn over with yarn A (photo 10), 16 sc with yarn A = 38 sts.

◄◄ When you crochet the 7 sc on round 17 with yarn B, do not forget to trap yarn A at the back with a handful of stitches to use it again at the end of the 7 sc. Do not pull on it to avoid misshaping the animal (it should remain quite supple at the rear).

Rnd 18: 12 sc with yarn A, 1 sc with the 1ˢᵗ yarn over with yarn A (photo 11) and the 2ⁿᵈ yarn over with yarn B (photo 12), 9 sc with yarn B (photo 13), 1 sc with the 1ˢᵗ yarn over with yarn B and the 2ⁿᵈ yarn over with yarn A, 15 sc with yarn A = 38 sts.

◄◄ When you crochet the 9 sc on round 18, do not forget to trap yarn A at the back with a handful of stitches to be able to use these at the end of the 9 sc. Do not pull on it to avoid misshaping the animal (it should remain quite supple at the rear).

Rnd 19: 12 sc with yarn A, 1 sc with the 1ˢᵗ yarn over of yarn A and the 2ⁿᵈ yarn over of yarn B, 10 sc with yarn B, 1 sc with the 1ˢᵗ yarn over with yarn B and the 2ⁿᵈ yarn over of yarn A, 14 sc with yarn A = 38 sts.

Rnd 20: 14 sc with yarn A, 9 sc with yarn B, 1 sc with the 1ˢᵗ yarn over with yarn B and the 2ⁿᵈ yarn over with yarn A, 14 sc with yarn A = 38 sts.

Rnd 21: 15 sc with yarn A, 1 sc with the 1ˢᵗ yarn over with yarn B and the 2ⁿᵈ yarn over with yarn A, 6 sc with yarn B, 2 sc with the 1ˢᵗ yarn over with yarn B and the 2ⁿᵈ yarn over with yarn A, 14 sc with yarn A = 38 sts.

Fasten off yarn B, then continue with yarn A.

7

8

9

10

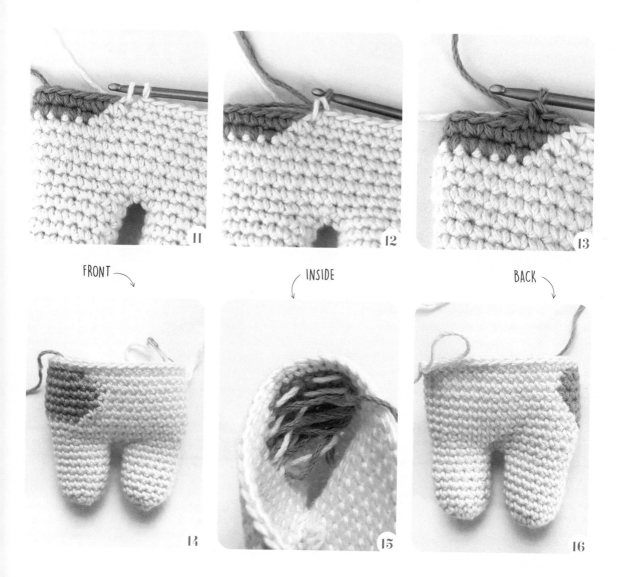

FRONT

INSIDE

BACK

Rnd 22: 38 sc (photos 14, 15 and 16).

Rnd 23: 2 sc, 1 dec, 16 sc, 1 dec, 16 dc = 36 sts.

Rnd 24 to 26: 36 sc (3 rnds).

Rnd 27: *4 sc, 1 dec* x 6 = 30 sts.

Rnd 28: 2 sc, 1 dec, [*6 sc, 1 dec* x 3], 2 sc = 26 sts.

Rnd 29: 2 sc, 1 dec, 11 sc, 1 dec, 9 sc = 24 sts.

↞ On the next round, you can crochet the arms to the body.

Rnd 30: 4 sc with one arm (for each sc, insert the hook in 1 st on the arm and 1 st on the body = 4 loops), 4 dec, 4 sc with the other arm (for each sc, insert the hook in 1 st on the arm and 1 st on the body = 4 loops), 4 dec = 16 sts.

Rnd 31: 13 inc, 2 sc, 1 inc = 30 sts.

Finish stuffing the body. Do not fasten off.

⋙ 4. THE HEAD ⋘

Rnd 32: 2 sc, 1 inc, [*4 sc, 1 inc* x 5] 2 sc = 36 sts.

Rnd 33: *5 sc, 1 inc* x 6 = 42 sts.

Rnd 34: 42 sc.

⋘ Please note that there are several colour changes for 10 rounds! At each colour change, the yarns should be hidden at the back (inside the piece). Do not cut them or pull them (to avoid misshaping the animal).

Rnd 35: 4 sc with yarn A, 2 sc with the 1st yarn over of yarn A and the 2nd yarn over with yarn B (for these 2 st), 8 sc with yarn B, 1 sc with the 1st yarn over of yarn B and the 2nd yarn over of yarn A, 27 sc with yarn A = 42 sts.

Rnd 36: 3 sc with yarn A, 2 sc with the 1st yarn over of yarn A and the 2nd yarn over with yarn B (for these 2 sts), 10 sc with yarn B, 1 sc with the 1st yarn over with yarn B and 2nd yarn over with yarn A, 26 sc with yarn A = 42 sts.

Rnd 37: 3 sc with yarn A, 1 sc with the 1st yarn over with yarn A and the 2nd yarn over with yarn B, 12 sc with yarn B, 1 sc with the 1st yarn over with yarn B and the 2nd yarn over with yarn A, 25 sc with yarn A = 42 sts.

Rnd 38: 4 sc with yarn A, 12 sc with yarn B, 1 sc with the 1st yarn over with yarn B and the 2nd yarn over with yarn A, 25 sc with yarn A = 42 sts.

Rnd 39: 5 sc with yarn A, 11 sc with yarn B, 1 sc with the 1st yarn over with yarn B and the 2nd yarn over with yarn A, 25 sc with yarn A = 42 sts.

Rnd 40: 6 sc with yarn A, 10 sc with yarn B, 1 sc with the 1st yarn over with yarn B and the 2nd yarn over with yarn A, 25 sc with yarn A = 42 sts.

Rnd 41: 7 sc with yarn A, 9 sc with yarn B, 1 sc with the 1st yarn over with yarn B and 2nd yarn over with yarn A, 25 sc with yarn A = 42 sts.

Rnd 42: 5 sc, 1 dec, 1 sc with yarn A, 4 sc, 1 dec, 2 sc with yarn B, 1 sc with the 1st yarn over with yarn B and the 2nd yarn over with yarn A, 2 sc, 1 dec, [*5 sc, 1 dec* x 3] with yarn A = 36 sts.

Rnd 43: 2 sc, 1 dec, 4 sc with yarn A, 1 dec, 3 sc with yarn B, 1 sc with the 1st yarn over with yarn B and the 2nd yarn over with yarn A, 1 dec, [*4 sc 1 dec* x 3], 2 sc with yarn A = 30 sts.

Rnd 44: 3 sc, 1 dec, 3 sc with yarn A, 1 dec, 1 sc with yarn B, 1 sc with the 1st yarn over with yarn B and the 2nd yarn over with yarn A, 1 sc, 1 dec, [*3 sc, 1 dec* x 3] with yarn A = 24 sts.

Fasten off yarn B, then continue with yarn A.

Rnd 45: 1 sc, 1 dec [*2 sc 1 dec* x 5] 1 sc = 18 sts.

Rnd 46: *1 sc, 1 dec* x 6 = 12 sts.

Finish stuffing the head.

Rnd 47: 6 dec = 6 sts.

Fasten off, leaving a 20 cm yarn tail to do an invisible finish. Weave in ends.

⋙ 5. THE SNOUT ⋘

With yarn A:

Rnd 1: 6 sc into a magic ring. Pull ring closed.

Rnd 2: *1 sc, 1 inc* x 3 = 9 sts.

Rnd 3: *2 sc, 1 inc* x 3 = 12 sts.

Finish with 2 sl st. Fasten off, leaving a 35 cm tail, do an invisible finish then use rest of length to attach the snout to the head.

Pin the snout to the head between rounds 32 and 36, ensuring it is central to the neck and giving it a triangular shape, with the tip towards the top. Attach using the yarn tail, partially stuffing before you reach the end.

Fasten off and weave in the ends.

↠ 6. THE EARS ↞

You can crochet the ears without stuffing them, one with yarn A and the other with yarn B.

Rnd 1: 6 sc into a magic ring. Pull ring closed.

Rnd 2: *1 sc, 1 inc* x 3 = 9 sts.

Rnd 3: *2 sc, 1 inc* x 3 = 12 sts.

Rnd 4: *3 sc, 1 inc* x 3 = 15 sts.

Rnd 5 to 9: 15 sc (5 rnds).

Finish off with 1 dc, leaving the rest of the stitches unworked.

Fasten off, leaving a 30 cm tail for attaching. Do an invisible finish.

Flatten the ears and pin them to the head sideways and flat, with the bottom of the base being at round 42 and the top at round 44 (6 stitches separate the ears on this round).

Stitch them tightly at the base, while closing off the opening (do not go around the entire ears, these should be flat).

Fasten off both ends and weave in.

↠ 7. THE EYES AND NOSE ↞

The eyes are positioned on a stitch at round 37 and are spaced 9 stitches apart. Using the black yarn, embroider 3 vertical points for each eye.

The nose should be at the top of round 1 of the snout. Embroider 4 vertical points.

Fasten off both ends and weave in.

ACKNOWLEDGEMENTS

A massive thank you to Nathalie, who trusted in me when writing this book, as well as Maud for your unstinting support and professionalism. I would also like to thank Véronique and Émilie for the wonderful graphics which match my universe so well.

Thanks to all of my fellow crochet colleagues. Thanks to your tutorials and videos, you have helped pass on your passion and get over my sticking points.

Thanks to my whole online community who follow me in my developments and which has continued to grow exponentially in recent months. Without you, I would not have been able to write this book.

A huge thank you to Marleen, Dounia, Marie and Vanessa for your tests. Your constant availability and insight were so valuable for me.

Thanks to all my friends and family.

Patrick and Léana, sincere thanks for supporting my mess, my lack of availability, and my constant obsession for my little animals... Thanks for your feedback and comments. Thanks for everything.

And, last but by no means least, thanks to you for holding this book! I sincerely hope that you like my little animals and that you have fun crocheting them.

Laurence

143

First published in Great Britain in 2024 by LOM ART, an imprint of
Michael O'Mara Books Limited
9 Lion Yard
Tremadoc Road
London SW4 7NQ

A CIP catalogue record for this book is available from the British Library.

This product is made of material from well-managed, FSC®-certified
forests and other controlled sources. The manufacturing processes
conform to the environmental regulations of the country of origin.

ISBN: 978-1-915751-24-9 in paperback print format

1 2 3 4 5 6 7 8 9 10

Director of publication: Isabelle Jeuge-Maynart and Ghislaine Stora
Editorial Director: Nathalie Viard
Publication: Maud Rogers
Artistic Director: Géraldine Lamy
Cover: Véronique Laporte
Graphic Design and layout: Émilie Laudrin
Production: Émilie Latour

Photos and sketches: Laurence Jourdan
Page and animal illustrations: Shutterstock

Printed and bound in China

www.mombooks.com

MIX
Paper | Supporting
responsible forestry
FSC® C010256